HOW TO SELL YOUR HOMEMADE CREATION

ALLAN H. SMITH

SUCCESS PUBLISHING

8084 Nashua Drive
Lake Park, Florida 33410

Illustrations by Don Trachsler

NEW ADDRESS:
2812 BAYONNE DR.
PALM BEACH GARDENS, FL 33410

Published in the United States of America
by SUCCESS PUBLISHING
8084 Nashua Drive, Lake Park, Florida 33410
© 1985 Allan H. Smith 2nd Printing 1986

Printed in the United States of America
Library of Congress Number 84-52239
ISBN 0-931113-02-4

DEDICATION

To Judith Louise Smith "POOCH." My pal, advisor and wife; without her understanding and love this book would not be worth doing.

PRESS ON

NOTHING IN THE WORLD CAN TAKE THE PLACE OF PERSISTANCE. TALENT WILL NOT; NOTHING IS MORE COMMON THAN UNSUCCESSFUL MEN WITH TALENT. GENIUS WILL NOT; UNREWARDED GENIUS IS ALMOST A PROVERB

EDUCATION ALONE WILL NOT; THE WORLD IS FULL OF EDUCATED DERELICTS. PERSISTENCE AND DETERMINATION ALONE ARE OMNIPOTENT.

INTRODUCTION

There are some 21 million American households that have a business at home, according to a survey by the AT&T Consumer Products. Of that number, 44% work solely at home, while the remaining 56% do a significant amount of their work there. As a group, the survey found at-home workers tend to be younger, better educated, and more affluent than office workers. Twice as many have college degrees and twice as many earn $40,000 a year or more.

My wife Judy and I have been in various home businesses for over 20 years. We have shared the failures and successes that have been part of the home-business industry. Working at home has many advantages. We work hard all our lives to have a comfortable place to live, grow and maybe raise a family. To be able to earn money as we enjoy our enviroment is a great accomplishment.

Surveys have found that over 60% of people who go to work every day strongly dislike their jobs. This might be part of the reason why we Americans try so hard to have it our way . . . our own business and in our own home.

I wrote this book as a result of the many questions I received when teaching courses on "How to start a business of your own." The large amount of capital it takes to rent a store, stock it, buy equipment discourages many from starting their own business.

Did you know that 97% of our nation's business is done by companies that employ 5 or less people and they employ 85% of the entire work force of America? See how important you and I are to the economy of the country. In Canada the figures are within plus or minus 10%. We are fortunate in this free world to have the opportunities to "have it our way."

This book is a collection of ideas, facts and suggestions. They are to help you SELL your creation. I like to call it a creation because it is probably done with your talent, ingenuity, enthusiasm, persistence and love. Every time I see the creations displayed at various shows I realize how clever we humans are. In fact, Judy must be getting tired of my repetitious remark, "I can't believe how talented people are!" You are those people, you have something to be proud of . . . your creation.

TABLE OF CONTENTS

CHAPTER ONE

WHAT DOES IT TAKE?

When you make that certain creation, a sense of pride and accomplishment surrounds you. You want the whole world to admire your talents and efforts. You also assume that others will buy every item produced. This is a good attitude to take. Many success books, philosophers, psychologists and counselors have said "What you think is what you will be." One of the most influencial books ever written, THINK AND GROW RICH by Napoleon Hill, stresses this philosophy. So many people are defeated by themselves, by their negative attitudes, or by their lack of self-confidence. Here are the highlights of THINK AND GROW RICH; it just might help motivate someone to go out and be ultra-successful.

A. THINK AND GROW RICH - The six principles you should have:

NOTES

1. DESIRE . . . you should acquire a picture of what you one day will become. (Close your eyes and picture what you want and what you will look like when you get it)

NEVER RETREAT OR LOOK BACK

If it is for MONEY, then:

a. Put down the exact amount you want to earn.

b. Determine what you will give in return. You have to make a commitment or sacrifice. Many times the sacrifices are not that demanding, but you MUST pay some dues. It could be in time, in accrued savings, time away from family, social events, hobbies or relaxing.

c. Establish a definite date by which you want to accomplish your money-goal (i.e. I will make $10,000 the first year from today September 30th, 1987).

d. BEGIN **AT ONCE** AND CREATE A PLAN FOR CARRY-ING OUT YOUR GOAL.

For Instance:

GOAL - TO MAKE $10,000 (after expenses) by September 30, 1987

START .... September 30, 1987

PRODUCT .... Hand-held puppets

NAME .... Goofus, Topsy, Muffin, Krumpy

PRICE .... $10⁰⁰ each

AMOUNT TO INVEST $5,000

SOURCE OF INVESTMENT .... Borrow on life insurance policy

PLACE OF OPERATION .... Converted area in garage

MARKET PROCEDURE .... Craft shows, mail order

ADVERTISING .... Classified ads in 4 publications

BUDGET .... See enclosed

SALES PROJECTION .... To make $10,000, I must sell 1,000.
For profit, expenses (budget of $3,500), I must sell another 350 puppets or 1350 in total, 110 a month or 3 a day. At this time, I can see my goal is a little too high, so I will modify it to making $5,000 the first year, and cut my expense budget to $1,500. This means I now have to sell 650 puppets in a year or about 50/month. This goal will not make me discouraged.

CRAFT SHOWS TO ATTEND .... etc., etc., etc.

You now have a clear picture of what you are doing and where you will be in a year. If you sell more than 650, then you will have accomplished MORE than expected.

NOTES

e. READ THIS STATEMENT TWICE A DAY . . . YOU CAN DO IT! You are just as talented as Xavier Roberts, the creator of the Cabbage Patch Kids and as imaginable as Jim Henson (Muppets creator). Don't EVER let anyone change this POSITIVE ATTITUDE.

3. AUTOSUGGESTION . . . the more you repeat your desires and goals, the more you will convince your inner sense that you will do it. It is just like programming a computer. As you repeat your desires the more you convince yourself to get moving, to stop procrastinating and goofing off.

4. SPECIALIZED KNOWLEDGE . . . I am not asking you to tear apart a Diesel motor and put it together again, although I'll bet some of you could, just asking you to do what you do the best . . ., CREATE! Obviously, if you do not have talent you will not be as successful. You may hire others or buy other products and promote them. Don't stop learning, if you have to take a night class, or buy another book to sharpen you skills, DO IT! We are just like the green plants in our kitchen, either growing or dying . . . to grow, learn more and expand your talents.

2

5. IMAGINATION . . . I just mentioned Cabbage Patch and the Muppets. Talk about imagination! How about Steve Spielberg, Star Wars, E.T. etc. and Walt Disney . . . what imagination. Usually the ultra-successful think up creations that are original, not copies. There are a lot of "copiers" who do make money though. Of course we all would like to come up with another Pet Rock or Hoola Hoop, — OOPS, gave away my age. NEVER STOP IMAGINING AND CREATING.

6. ORGANIZED PLANNING . . . as we discussed in the first principle, you must be organized:

   a. Have a procedure that will accomplish a particular GOAL.

   b. Have a budget.

   c. Break your goals into "bite-sized pieces." You must have a list that will guide you to your goal each month, each week and a daily goal list.

NOTES

3

TIME TO PICK THE DAISIES

It's written by someone looking back at life and wishing it could be different. I share it with you in the hope that it will help you live a life that you won't wish you could rewrite. It's called, "I'd pick more daisies."

"If I had my life to live over, I'd try to make more mistakes next time.

I would relax.

I would limber up.

I would be sillier than I have been this trip.

I Know of very few things I would take seriously.

I would be crazier.

I would be less hygienic.

I would climb more mountains, swim more rivers, and watch more sunsets.

I would eat more ice cream and less beans.

I would have more actual troubles and fewer imaginary ones.

You see, I am one of those people who lives prophylactically and sensibly and sanely, hour after hour, day after day.

Oh, I have had my moments, and, if I had to do it over again, I'd have more of them.

In fact, I'd try to have nothing else.

Just moments, one after another, instead of living so many years ahead each day.

I have been one of those people who never go anywhere without a thermometer, a hot water bottle, a gargle, a raincoat and parachute.

If I had it to do over again, I would go places and do things and travel lighter than I have.

If I had my life to live over, I would start barefooted earlier in the Spring and stay that way later in the Fall.

I would play hooky more.

I wouldn't make such good grades except by accident.

I would ride on more merry-go-rounds.

I'd pick more daisies."

Anonymous.

4

B. SOME AREAS OF CONSIDERATION

Before we get into specifics, may I share a few basics with you — ideas that may save you money and time later.

NOTES

1. Is your product something the public needs?

2. Is there a demand for it, is it unusual, unique or difficult to get somewhere else?

3. Can you tie up the source of materials for your product and reduce competition? REMEMBER . . . as soon as you succeed you will have copy-cats who will try to share YOUR success.

4. Don't depend on ONE item, develop a line of products.

5. THINK IT OVER CAREFULLY BEFORE STARTING

6. Search out reliable suppliers and stick with them.

7. Try to figure the shipping in on the retail price. A recent survey stated that 65% of consumers said they would buy if there were no additional shipping charges.

8. ALWAYS offer a money-back guarantee . . . It usually amounts to ½% of your total sales even with a quality product. That means one out of 200 wil ask for his money back, BUT many more will buy with that feeling of confidence.

9. If using mail-order, make the price one bill, as many will send cash through the mail (i.e. $5, $10, not $7.83).

10. Low retail price items will not generate profit; it costs too much to promote and ship.

11. The THREE RULE — don't advertise unless you can do it three consecutive times. It takes a consumer's time to determine IF they want the item . . . and IF you are legitimate.

12. ALWAYS sell the BENEFIT(S) the consumers will get IF they buy your product.

13. Consider using a bonus or a free item.

14. NEVER accept selling by C.O.D. . . . and do not mention it in your ads.

15. Accept checks . . . very few bounce.

16. Avoid using BILL ME on order forms.

17. Make immediate refunds.

NOTES

6

C. DON'TS

It is always better to learn from other people's mistakes than from your own. It is less costly. Again, I always like to remain positive and have a bright outlook on life. These negatives are to help you to have that successful journey that you WILL HAVE!

NOTES

7

Don't:

1. Use Enterprise after your business name, it is a sign of an amateur, which of course we are, but don't want others to know it.

2. Use bulky items that will cost a lot to ship. In one of my classes, I had a lady who hand made wood doll beds. She found it cost more to package and mail than to make.

3. Expect a profit on anything less than $20 shipped by mail.

4. Be underfinanced.

5. Advertise without testing first.

6. Make a lot of items until you are sure that other people like it as well as you do.

7. Sell without a Tax Number.

8. Bank without a company account.

9. Do business without a company name.

10. Produce an inferior product. We all have attended craft shows and observed craft products that should not be for sale, but who has the heart to tell that person who has spent so many hours of work to produce it.

11. Pack your product in an unimaginative, dull package.

12. Overprice or underprice your product.

13. Forget to guarantee money back.

NOTES

14. Charge shipping and handling. If possible, absorb them in the Retail price.

15. Sell without insurance for product liability.

16. Refuse to guarantee money-back returns.

17. Copy others.

18. Advertise just once — three is better.

19. Refuse to accept checks.

20. Do business without having MasterCard/Visa number.

21. Turn down networking with others.

22. Use "Bill Me" on order forms.

23. Start charging or charge accounts.

24. Lower your price, unless previously agreed (i.e. discounts).

25. Give away your products, unless they can help promote, sell or influence reviews or buyers.

26. Forget to include an indentifying label on EVERY item.

27. Depend on producing only ONE item.

28. Expect ot make it overnight.

29. Forget to patent, copyright or trademark your product.

30. Allow others to copy you without a fight.

8

31. Take on partners unless necessary.

32. Work in an unproductive atmosphere. Have your own spot, even if it means a closet, basement, garage, barn or attic.

33. Allow yourself to be disturbed while you are creating. Soon others will respect your time and privacy.

34. Allow agents, professionals, wholesalers, customers, friends, family or others to take advantage of you.

35. Start your venture without a plan and a budget.

36. Become discouraged with failures. They are only opportunities that have not worked out.

37. Spend money on new equipment if you can borrow or lease.

38. Expect "instant profits."

39. Do it if it is a chore, boring or uninteresting.

40. Ignore customers' requests and questions. Answer immediately.

41. Be unorganized. It will cost you money in the long run.

42. Take out all the profits. Reinvest in yourself and your talents to become even MORE successful.

43. Stop learning. Take other courses, read books, ask questions, attend shows and seminars.

44. Brag about your successes. Others will copy you, not believe you, or be envious . . . play it cool.

45. Belittle other crafts people or competition.

46. Hire others, unless you have a good grasp on business procedures and interpersonal skills.

NOTES

47. Ignore your friends and family completely. They also are a product of you and have to be successful . . . but don't let them prevent your expression of talent by doing what you love.

48. Forget to "network" and share your knowledge with other craftpeople.

49. Become obsessed with one area of products. Consider other ways to express your creativity.

SUCCESS OR FAILURE IN BUSINESS IS CAUSED MORE BY THE MENTAL ATTITUDE THAN BY MENTAL CAPACITIES.

NOTES

D. GETTING ORGANIZED

Not taking the time to work out a system for getting regular chores done or filing away important pieces of information can make simple tasks take twice as long.

Many business analysts attribute lack of capital and poor management as the biggest causes of business failures. Good management is the control of time and being organized.

Today — Personal Philosophy

Today is here. I will start with a smile and resolve
to be agreeable. I will not criticize.
I refuse to waste my valuable time.

Today in one thing I know I am equal with all
others — Time.
All of us draw the same salary in seconds, minutes
and hours.

Today I am determined to study to improve myself,
for tomorrow I may be wanted, and must not be found lacking.

Today I will stop saying, "If I had time."
I know I never will "find time" for anything.
If I want time, I must make it.

Today I will act toward other people as though this might be my
last day on earth.
I will not wait for tomorrow.
Tomorrow never comes.

10

If you think you don't have time to be organized, chances are you've let chaos get the upper hand. Chaos may be perfected for romantic poets, but it doesn't work in business, especially if the business is your own. THE TRUTH IS, YOU DON'T HAVE TIME **NOT** TO BE ORGANIZED. If you are entering the competitive world of selling to the consumer you must become organized.

A major university studied alumni 20 years after graduation. Only 3% had established clear lifetime aims or goals. This 3% had accomplished incredibly more than the others.

Many of you could write a book on efficiency and how to control time. Still some need guidelines and motivation to get more done in less time.

Let's share some basic principles that may help you accomplish more in less time. After all time is money when you work for yourself.

1. TAKE CONTROL OF YOUR WORK AREA/DESK

a. Collect all the scraps of paper you've accumulated: telephone messages, recipes, old bills, advertisements, bright ideas scribbled on cocktail napkins and "things to do" lists.

b. Remove ALL reference materials and place them in a reference area.

c. Remove all unnecessary items, such as dog photos, pictures of your golf/shopping/social friends, plastic flowers, ornate figurines from Disneyworld, pen/pencil holders, that haven't worked in three years, complex paperclips, rubber bands, eraser holders, etc. These should be in a drawer, thrown out or placed on a shelf that doesn't produce money for you.

d. NOW! doesn't it look better? Your mind will not unconsciously perceive these non-productive distractions.

e. Make sure you have good lighting. A 40-watt bulb hanging overhead will not do. A flourescent desk/work light will not strain your eyes.

f. If you sit, have a comfortable chair, not a folding metal chair with rusty legs. This can prolong your efficiency and your back . . . it will prevent fatigue. If you stand, make sure you are standing on a rubber or thick mat/rug. This can prevent fatigue and cold if it is winter.

g. Vetilation. There should be fresh air circulating, especially if you smoke. You may need a fan, heater or portable air conditioner.

NOTES

11

h. Materials. Have them handy. The easiest is having close proximity of your work items. NOT STORED ON THE DESK OR WORK AREA! Put a cabinet, file cabinet, bookshelf, drawers or suspend them from the ceiling.

i. PRIVACY. Try, and I do say try, to have a quiet secluded work area. Yes, it is difficult with kids, dogs, delivery men, bill collectors and friends bothering you. I finally moved into the garage after trying the living room, the den and bedroom. It took a little paneling, doors and a rug that we replaced from the family room. They only trouble is that the kids and dogs like it as much as I do. It has got to be a meeting place ESPECIALLY if I am trying to write. I'll take it though; it gives me privacy if I feel like working late into the night. (The worst thing for some people is to hear the clicking of the typewriter constantly.)

j. POWER AND UTILITY SOURCES. If you need electrical outlets, water, sinks, telephones or whatever, INSTALL them. Try to save steps if possible. I've seen some great work areas in cellars, garages, attics, barns and porches.

2. KEEP IT CLEAN. Pick up the trash, papers, garbage AFTER each work period. It will give you a fresh outlook when you start the next time. I have done consulting for a lot of firms and it amazes me how some people can create anything with the amount of confusion and dirt they surround themselves with.

3. HAVE A PLAN. Even if you make a list on toilet paper sheets, make some kind of work schedule for yourself EACH day. Pick up a chalk board or make your own list each day . . . but DO IT. Why do they have rudders on sail boats? . . . to guide them to a destination. If you have not a plan or a list of goals, then you will just drift along each day and let other people and other things control your time and efforts. Just like a boat without a rudder.

NOTES

4. ELIMINATE TIME WASTERS . . . The TEN biggies are:

   a. Lack of organization

   b. Lack of priorities

   c. Too much work

   d. Lack of motivation

   e. Improper procedures

   f. Bad communications

   g. Doing jobs or tasks others could do cheaper or more efficiently

   h. Shortage of time

   i. People interruptions

   j. Procrastinating

A well organized person can do more in three hours than some in a whole day. The average office worker wastes 5½ hours a week by not being organized.

1. SEPARATE WORK and HOME . . . this can be tough, but here are some suggestions:

   a. Have a particular area for work.

   b. Let it be known to others in the household that you would like privacy. A subtle hint a few times should do the trick

   c. Have a schedule and stick by it.

   d. STAY AWAY FROM THE REFRIGERATOR.

   e. Reward yourself for doing so much in so much time - a cup of coffee, a cigarette, a glass of juice, a sandwich, a trip to the bathroom, a phone call or just day dreaming.

   f. Respect the rights of others and they will respect your rights.

   g. If you need a separate phone and the business can support one, then it will pay off in the long run.

2. LEARN TO BE SELF DISCIPLINED.

   a. Set a list each day and finish it OR add it on to the next day.

   b. Start work immediately.

   c. Do the most unpleasant task first . . . that phone call, the difficult letter, that hard painting, the difficult mold, etc.

   d. If you work at home like a lot of us do . . . STAY AWAY FROM THE FRIDGE . . . you can really put on pounds.

   e. REWARD yourself for accomplishments.

   f. The more control you have over yourself, the more control you have over your time. If your time will be used wisely, your successes will come faster.

NOTES

CHAPTER TWO

PLANNING AND BUDGETING YOUR VENTURE

Just like a computer, car, sailboat or person, your business must be guided along. It is unbelievable how many people go into business with little forethought and organization. When you sit down to create, you must first plan what you are going to make. You must have a design, buy the materials and find the time.

NOTES

A PRAYER FOR TODAY

This is the beginning of a new day. God has given me this day to use as I will. I can waste it — or use it for good, but what I do today is important, because I am exchanging a day of my life for it! When tomorrow comes, this day will be gone forever, leaving in its place something that I have traded for it. I want it to be gain, and not loss; good and not evil; success, and not failure; in order that I shall not regret the price I have paid for it.

Author unknown

A. CREATING A DESIGN (A PLAN)

Where do I start, when, with what, how and when will it be finished: Let's make it simple. Take a clean sheet of paper, copy my suggestion or modify it to your liking. I have known many business owners, corporate presidents, store manager, teachers etc. The SUCCESS-FUL ones use this type of planning or one much like it.

Action (what you are going to do)	Who will do it	Materials Needed	Cost	Tobe Done by	Finished
Create a name	Linda	n/a (not applicable)	n/a	Mar. 10	Mar. 9
Form a plan	Linda Joan	n/a	n/a	Mar. 10	Mar. 8
Plan a budget	Linda Joan	references	n/a	Mar. 15	Mar. 17
Order labels, stationery, calling cards, etc.	Joan	designs, names	$200	Mar. 20	Mar. 19
Set up office	Linda and Joan/ husbands	office materials rugs, desks, etc.	$350	Mar. 30	Apr. 3
Order materials	Linda and Joan	(see enclosed list)	$942	Mar. 30	Apr. 15
Determine marketing strategy	Linda and Joan	references	n/a/	Apr. 10	Apr. 11
Set up Bookkeeping System	Linda and Joan/ husbands	references	n/a	Apr. 10	Apr. 11
Accountant, Attorney	Joan	references	n/a	Apr. 10	Apr. 11
Order packaging materials	Linda	Bags, boxes wrapping paper, tape	$150	Mar. 30	Mar. 28
Check on insurance needed	Joan	n/a	n/a	Mar. 30	Mar. 25
Determine advertising plan	Linda and Joan	references	n/a	Apr. 15	Apr. 17
Test the Product	Linda & Joan	past actions	n/a	May 25	May 25
Create & order adver- tising materials	Linda and Joan	brochures	$75	May 1	May 1
Evaluate results so far	Linda & Joan	past actions	n/a	May 25	May 25
Formulate new products	Linda and Joan	references	n/a	May 30	May 30

etc., etc.

NOTES

15

As you can observe, Linda and Joan now have a guide to help them start their business professionally. The chances of success are much greater with a plan such as this.

B.   DESIGNING A BUDGET

How much money you have and how you will spend it.

Linda and Joan are sisters. They have an automatic trust relationship. They live within two blocks of each other, are married and have small children. They have an urgent need to find recognition by creating something themselves. They do not want to work for someone else to find that extra income that can pay a lot of bills. For years they have sewed, learning the art from their mother. Linda makes most of her families' clothes; Joan likes to make gift and craft wear for others and to sell at the local church bazaar held once a year. One day they decided to "pool" their talents and make aprons and affix personal names to them. They started attracting attention at a school craft fair. Since then they have had a few requests to make more for people to give as gifts. Linda had a large garage with heat and good ventilation. They decided to have their husbands make them a workshop office for their business. Joan could bring her pre-school children over to Linda's while they were creating. Linda's children are in the elementary grades. Now they have to find the money and determine when, where and how they can spend it.

Both girls will contribute $5000 to the business for a total of $10,000. Here is the way they went about budgeting their monies.

To get started (for the first six months)

Office equipment	$150
Office supplies	100
Legal expenses	500
Licenses	50
Insurance	150
Printing	50
Packaging materials	135
Postal expenses	50
Material	1000
Advertising	1500
Marketing materials (brochures, inserts, slingers)	150
Fees for shows, fairs etc.	200
Utilities (phone, extra electricity)	400
Misc.	200

$4635

16

Now Linda and Joan have an idea of how much it will cost and what resources they have. It makes arriving at business decisions a lot easier. YOU MUST HAVE A BUDGET AND A PLAN!!!

CHAPTER THREE

NAMING AND
PRICING YOUR CREATION

"YOU NEVER HAVE A SECOND CHANCE AT A FIRST IMPRESSION" . . . your name, price and package design must be attractive and "shout out" BUY ME! BUY ME!

NOTES

NAMING

Here are some suggestions that may help you when naming the product or your business.

1. IT SHOULD BE ORIGINAL. If you are creative enough to make that product, then it will be easy to name it. R. David Thomas named his product after his daughter and called it Wendy's Hamburgers; so did Mr. Benz name his car after his daughter Mercedes. Henry Panasci, Jr., named his first store after his wife's name. He now has over 100 Fay Drug Stores. You will have to do some research and make sure someone else has not used the name.

2. IT SHOULD BE EASY TO PRONOUNCE. Yes, I know that a French or Spanish name is exotic BUT will it help to sell the product? Many use their own names: Judi's Dolls, Ellen's Aprons, Products by the Browns, Original Creations by Joan, Alterations by Sam, Dog-gone Clothes by Fido, etc.

3. It should describe the product, the service, or the function of the company. Sally's Blouses, Grandma's Great Kitchen Helpers, Mother Bones Dolls, Muffin's Magic, Pooch's Pals, etc.

4. IT SHOULD BE EASILY REMEMBERED AND RECOGNIZED. it may pay to have a logo or design to fortify the name. You'll notice more and more companies using logos. Be creative and design your own calling card, label, invoice, note paper, etc. People seem to remember pictures and names longer than either alone.

NOTES

5. TRY TO COORDINATE THE NAME, THE PRODUCT OR THE SERVICE IF POSSIBLE. If you attend craft shows, examine the originality of products, labels and signs.

6. REMEMBER that sometimes the package name can help sell the product BETTER than the product itself!

7. If you are a corporation, then you must REGISTER YOUR BUSINESS name with your state. It must be one of a kind.

8. SHORTER IS USUALLY BETTER. In a given space, short names have more impact than long ones.

9. KEEP TO ONE, two or three phonetic sounds per name. When people embrace a name, they usually shorten it . . . "Bud" for Budweiser, "Coke" for Coca Cola.

10. LOOK FOR GOOD SPEECH. Will it stand out in typical spoken English? We have certain styles of speech. We usually like it short, sweet and simple.

11. LOOK FOR GOOD VISIBILITY. Find ways to have your name STAND OUT in print . . . phonetic spellings-Compaq for compact, Exxon, NITE, for night. Each time a customer thinks of these nonconformists spellings, they think of you.

NOTES

PRICING

This is an important aspect of marketing your product. You must sell it high enough to make money and low enough so others will buy it.

An old rule of thumb is to double your cost. Manufacturers

NOTES

figure ten times cost. Many retailers mark a product up only a third or forty percent. Supermarkets have a gross profit in the teens and a net in the 1 and 2's. Let's take a look at what constitutes costs, markups, profits, nets, and some other terms with which you will come in contact. Many of these you will use yourself, some when you deal with wholesalers, distributors and retailers.

ACCOUNTS RECEIVABLE. . . that is the money owed to you.

ACCOUNTS PAYABLE . . . the money you owe to others

ASSETS . . . after what you owe is deducted, the rest is assets.

BAD DEBT . . . that old receivable that you can't collect

BANKRUPTCY . . . when you can't make it, you can get the federal government to protect you from any further hassels.

BOOK VALUE . . . same as net worth, subtract assets from liabilities.

C.O.D. . . . cash on delivery . . . money on the barrelhead.

CAPITALIZATION . . . the amount of "seed" money or original money you or others invest in a business.

CASH-FLOW . . . how much cash over and above your debts or payables you have.

COLLATERAL . . . how much you have in assets in stocks, property, bank accounts that you could use to borrow on.

CORPORATIONS . . . the full corporation and the subchapter S, government-regulated and costly.

COGS (COSTS OF GOODS SOLD) . . . the amount the entire goods cost to put together - the thread, material, label, box etc.

DEPRECIATION . . . usually real estate and equipment depreciates so much each year, much like us-we get older and slower every year -but we may be more effective with slow motion.

DISCOUNTS . . . what the customers look for when they buy your product. Many times suppliers give a 2% discount if the bill is paid within a certain time.

20

EQUITY . . . how much you or your investor has in the business.

F.O.B. (FREIGHT ON BOARD) . . . that means you pay for the shipping of the product from its origination.

FISCAL YEAR . . . year's calendar year, may be set when the business is started or when ever convenient.

KEYSTONE . . . used by jewelry stores, meaning double the cost.

LIABILITY . . . besides employing your Uncle's step-son, it's what you owe from loans or payables.

NET WORTH . . . deduct liabilities from assets and you've got it!

OVERHEAD . . . what it costs to operate your business, rent, heat, light, taxes, interest and employing your uncle's step-son.

RECEIVABLES . . . what is owed to you.

CHAPTER 11 . . . The step before bankruptcy. Protection from being sued by your credits while you are reorganizing or refinancing.

NOTES

21

WHEN WE ARE WRONG HELP US LEARN BY OUR MISTAKES AND CHANGE, AND WHEN WE ARE RIGHT, LET'S MAKE IT EASY TO LIVE WITH US.

Pricing can make or break you. If the price is wrong, all the other work and effort means little. It could be too low priced OR too high. Let's share some experiences and knowledge about prices and pricing.

1. You will receive more QUALIFIED buyers by charging a nominal fee for a sample than by giving it away. People seem to regard its value higher if they have to exert some effort or spend some monies to obtain something.

2. Giving away your creation to friends or relatives does little to increase your popularity or reputation. You could have a "courtesy" discount for relatives, clergy, teachers, professionals, etc. I would suggest no more than 10 or 20% AND STICK TO IT.

3. FORMULATE A PRICE LIST AT ONCE . . . example

   one . . . . $20.00 each
   two to six . . . . 17.70 each
   six to 20 . . . . 15.00
   20-50 . . . . 12.50
   50-100 . . . . 10.00

4. STIPULATE YOUR HANDLING, SHIPPING or MAILING charges.

   Shipped Postpaid
   $1.50 s/h (shipping and handling)
   F.O.B. WEST PALM BEACH . . . that means whatever it costs to ship it from W.P.B. to wherever.

NOTES

5. NEVER, NEVER SHIP C.O.D. You'll find some will refuse to accept the order and you will be stuck with freight BOTH ways.

6. INCLUDE APPROPRIATE TAXES. If your state or county has a sales tax, then charge it to those in YOUR state to whom you ship or sell. You should have a tax number; avoid it now and you will have to do it later. REMEMBER you are going to be successful. Not obtaining a number and collecting taxes is admission of not wanting to be bigger and profitable.

7. MARK EVERY ITEM with a price tag. Make it hard or impossible to remove.

8. CODE YOUR COST. As you grow larger and expand (business-wise that is) into more products, you may hire others and forget your cost. If you handle other people's goods, or have consignments then the label should have your cost included. Here are some basic business codes . . . Each letter represents a number . . .

22

1	2	3	4	5	6	7	8	9	0
R	E	P	U	B	L	I	C	A	N
D	E	M	O	C	R	A	T	E	S
U	S	A	M	E	R	I	C	O	D

You can make up any code you wish. If a product costs $1.00, the first code would read RNN. If it costs $19.83 then RACP. You could even include the date of acquisition. The label could read $22.50 REBN 6/4 . . . selling of course for $22.50, costs $12.50 and was made or bought June 1984.

9. DISCOUNT OLD, WORN, OUTDATED MERCHANDISE. The name of the game is TURNOVER — the more you can turn over your products, the more money or profit you will make. If you keep an item for more than one year in stock, you have lost money. If money is worth about 15% to borrow, that's about 1¼% per month. By keeping a product for a year, you have lost the earning power of the money you have invested PLUS the money you already have spent. If you have a product for a year, discount it 50% to close it out, get rid of it. If you still have it after another six months take another 50% off. If after two years you STILL have the dust gatherer GIVE IT AWAY . . . just to inventory dust and move it costs money. Some shoppes that have numerous sale items have put them in a grab-bag for 99¢/$2.99 even $9.99 and sold everything they could bag. Ever see the SURPRISE packages that catalog mail orders offer? These are "dog" items that they can't sell. They have put them in an attractive box and offered them to us at GREAT savings . . . $25 worth of gifts for $5.99. It works!!

10. TEST THE PRICE. Put different prices on the same product and offer it at different places at different times. See what the traffic will bear. You may find the higher price will sell better. If you are going to try mail-order then try different TEASER-ADS with different prices.

NOTES

11. TRY TO COMPARE. What are others getting for the same kind of item? Of course we look at the Cabbage Patch Kids and nothing can justify the $150 to 300 price tag BUT they line up in Cleveland, Georgia to buy them. We all have put many hours of labor, sweat and love into our creations; our price should re-imburse us.

12. DETERMINE YOUR WORTH. You will work initially for pennies, as you become recognized and accepted, your time should be worth more. There are times when you can work on your craft while watching TV, talking to a friend, waiting for an appointment or riding in a car. These are "bonus hours," doing two things at once. BUT you still should determine what you are worth. The minimum you are worth is $3.35/hour . . . you can get a job anytime for that. If it takes 10 hours to construct your creation, then you already have $33.50 into it WITHOUT counting materials and overhead.

13. MATERIAL COSTS. Figure everything you use in the product . . . material, thread, buttons, labels, packing materials . . . NOT advertising or marketing costs.

14. OVERHEAD COSTS. Let's be honest; if you are doing it at home, then your overhead could be very little . . . maybe sewing machine repairs, a bottle of aspirin, or a little more electricity. You may have to set up more elaborate quarters such as remodeling an attic, basement, garage or barn, THEN your costs have to be calculated.

23

Some of the overhead expenses may include.

* Utilities, phone, electric, etc.

* Rent, if you are not at home

* Liability insurance, for your products, and working area(s)

* Transportation, car expense. You may deduct your expenses incurred gathering goods, delivering etc. WATCH IT, IRS loves to doubt you and will many times call for an audit if these expenses are large.

* Maintenance to the machinery, car, building, etc.

* Cleaning and repairs

* Shipping

* Advertising, marketing

* Office equipment and supplies

* Employees

* Taxes

* Legal expenses

15. WHOLESALERS AND DISTRIBUTORS. You may have to offer them a deeper discount. When I published my first book, I found that I had to discount it 60% to one distributor. They sold thousands, but the profit was minimal. Again you will have to play by ear or establish a price list of wholesalers and distributors in the beginning.

NOTES

24

CHAPTER FOUR

TESTING THE PRODUCT

As I previously stated, a certain pride and satisfaction comes from a handmade creation. You must determine IF others think the same. IF they do, then you have a good chance of selling it to them. How do we find out if it is acceptable?

NOTES

STEP NO. 1

1. Is it well made, free from defects, errors, frayed ends, soiled areas, etc.?

2. Can it be displayed so others can see it, preferably so others can touch or feel it. You could have one for display, some items such as egg-art items must be shown with caution.

3. Do you have an idea of price to charge? (We will go into this in detail in later chapters)

These three questions should be answered to get started.

These are some ideas for you to TEST your product BEFORE spending money or making too many.

STEP NO. 2

Investigate the various craft, sewing, etc., books on the newstand or at the library. The library usually will have ALL and more of the popular books for you to review. Notice the different products, the method of advertising, price, etc.

CONSUMER MAGAZINE AND AGRI-MEDIA, published by Standard Rate and Data Service Inc., 3004 Glenview Rd., Wilmette, IL 60091, lists most magazines published. The book consists of many volumes, some for radio/TV, some for newspapers. You will find many magazines you never knew existed that will give you ideas. These magazines will have features and ads on similar items such as yours. Compare prices, style, quality, quantity, etc. Are you in line or barking up the wrong tree?

NOTES

Attend, as you probably already have, craft shows. Has someone else made the exact same thing and is selling it for half what you want to sell it for?

Investigate craft stores and observe the same thing.

If you still are confident that your creation has passed these basic tests then follow the next step.

STEP NO. 3

1. Ask your family members and friends for their HONEST opinions. Don't just ask if they like the product, be specific. Would they buy it if someone else made it? How much would they pay for it? Do they have any suggestions, positive or negative? Every time I teach a class, I always end it with a questionnaire.

> WHAT DID YOU LIKE THE MOST ABOUT THE CLASS?
>
> WHAT DID YOU LIKE THE LEAST ABOUT THE CLASS?
>
> WHAT SUGGESTIONS CAN YOU GIVE TO MAKE IT BETTER?
>
> RATE THE INSTRUCTOR (1-10) _____

You could adapt these questions to your product.

> WHAT DO YOU LIKE THE BEST ABOUT THE PRODUCT?
>
> WHAT DO YOU LIKE THE LEAST ABOUT THE PRODUCT?
>
> WHAT SUGGESTIONS CAN YOU GIVE TO MAKE IT BETTER?
>
> _____
>
> _____
>
> RATE THE PRICE (1-10) _____
>
> RATE THE QUALITY (1-10) _____

Many people will write more critically than giving an honest verbal evaluation. (see example)

NOTES

2. Ask a craft specialist or store owner for their evaluation of your product/creation. You may expect more direct honest answers from them. Have the five questions typed on a 3×5 card and ask them to fill it out.

3. Ask a fellow craftperson's opinion.

"THE MOST IMPORTANT ADVICE IS TO TAKE THE ADVICE AND COMMENTS GIVEN.

If you are still receiving positive feedback, and have very few adjustments to make, then you are ready for the next step.

STEP NO. 4

1. Seek out local craft fairs, church bazaars, school and church boutiques. Set up a booth with your creation featured. If you feel that you do not have enough to attract buyers, then team up with another person or persons. These low cost shows will give you a great TEST for your creation. (Refer to the chapter on How to Sell Successfully at a Craft Show.)

2. Carefully examine what has happened at the "show."

HERE IS AN EXAMPLE OF A "TEST" card you can use. A quick printer can do a professional job for very little money. Have them set four on a page so you can save more. A card is better than paper. Notice that there is an option for the person to include name and address. You may even have the other side imprinted with your name and address. The person then has the choice of sending it back to you via the mail. You should include one with every product you sell. The return information will be invaluable to you when making other decisions. The little cost of this type of testing may save large dollars in promoting the wrong product, the wrong price, color, style or whatever.

NOTES

SEW WHAT CREATIONS

WHAT DID I LIKE ABOUT THE PRODUCT ————————

————————————————————————————————

WHAT CAN WE DO TO IMPROVE THE PRODUCT ————

————————————————————————————————

————————————————————————————————

PLEASE RATE THE QUALITY (1-10) ——————

PLEASE RATE THE PRICE (1-10) ——————

NAME (optional) ————————————————

ADDRESS ——————————————————

————————————————————————————————

SEW WHAT CREATIONS
1224 Main Street
Anytown, U.S.A. 12345

28

a. How many did I sell?

b. What did it cost to rent the space?

c. Did I have enough?

d. What comments did I receive to improve my creation?

e. Was the price right?

f. What whould I do to increase sales the next time?

3. Evaluate the answers and determine if the public is "excited" enough about your creation to go ahead with making and selling more?

These low-cost TESTS will help you to make some creative and productive decisions and PREVENT you from making costly mistakes.

4. Make sure you have evaluated the market, that you are presenting the right product in the right area at the right time. Sounds tough, well it is . . . this is the secret of making money, having the right thing at the right price at the right place at the right time.

NOTES

29

NOTES

30

CHAPTER FIVE
100 POSSIBLE SOURCES FOR MATERIALS

To make a decent profit on your product you must be able to buy your materials at the right price. It is surprising the wide range of prices you will find. When I went shopping for prices to print this book, I found some printers that were two and three times higher than the lowest bidder. You have to do some investigating, some question-asking and some research to find the best prices.

Listed are some suggestions, sources and books that will make it easier for you:

1. FIRST, create and identify. You must have an authentic business to have others sell you wholesale.

    a. Have a business and/or product name

    b. Register this name with the proper agency (usually the county)

    c. Obtain a tax number with your State agency. This is one of the more obvious ways to obtain authenticity.
    Use this tax number to save not paying tax when you buy supplies. You must then, of course, charge tax.

    d. Have calling cards and/or stationery

    e. Be PATIENT AND PERSISTENT. . . always use your business stationery and type, not hand write, communications.

    f. Have order forms for your supplies.

    g. Have a bank account under the name of the company you use.

2. When starting out, combine your needs and ask for a discount from any supplier you're using, most of the time they will honor your request in hopes that you will be a bigger account.

3. For toy, hobby and craft supplies . . . Play things Directory ($3) 51 Madison Ave., New York, N.Y. 10010

4. Obtain Yellow Page Directories. For those in your area code they will be FREE. For other major cities where wholesale companies exist, the charge is minimal.

NOTES

5. HOMEMADE MONEY over 500 valuable information-by-mail resources - by Barbara Brabec - Success Publishing, Box 10632, Riviera Beach, Florida 33404 - $12.95.

6. THOMAS REGISTER OF AMERICAN MANUFACTURERS, at your library will list ALL of the sources.

7. If you belong to an organization, club or association, combine your needs OR use their name to add CLOUT to your requests.

8. Watch your newspapers AND the papers of near-by cities for sewing business going out of business and/or closeout sales.

9. APPAREL INDUSTRY MAGAZINE 6226 Vineland Ave., N. Hollywood, Ca. 91006. This is a national directory of apparel suppliers and contractors. (NOTE: always write on your business stationery and request catalogs, magazines, R & D data and prize lists)

10. NATIONAL NEEDLEWORK ASSOCIATION, INC. is a great source of information. It publishes NATIONAL NEEDLEWORK NEWS and sponsors trade shows . . . mail for more info.

11. CREATIVE PRODUCTS . . . FREE subscription if you prove authenticity . . . Box 584, Lake Forest, IL 60046 — GREAT SOURCES FOR SEWING PRODUCTS.

12. HOW TO MARKET YOUR HOMEMADE CREATION - many money saving idea . . . many shortcuts and time saving marketing methods . . . $11.95 Success Publications . . . Box 10632, Riviera Beach, FL 33404.

NOTES

13. SEW BUSINESS . . . a must for retailers in home-sewing, for quilting and needlework merchandise. Box 1331, Ft. Lee, N.J. 07024.

14. SEW NEWS . . . the newspaper for people who sew . . . 208 S. Main St., Seattle, SA 98104 . . . Loaded with money-saving ideas.

15. CATALOG SOURCES FOR CREATIVE PEOPLE by Margaret Boyd/over 2000 mail order sources . . . Success Publishing, Box 10632, Riviera Beach, FL 33404 $7.95.

16. SEWING FOR PROFITS . . . $10 . . . Success Publishing Box 10632, Riviera Beach, FL 33040 . . . Many ways to save money when going into business for yourself . . .

17. SEW AND SAVE SOURCE BOOK . . . By Margaret Boyd . . . 1500 mail order sources for creative and general sewing supplies . . . many wholesale . . . $11.45 . . . Success Publishing, 10632, Riviera Beach, FL 33404.

18. SOLO SLIDE . . . wholesale source, FREE brochure for hand and machine sewing notions . . . 77 Tosca Dr., Box 528, Stoughton, MA 02072.

19. Designers fabrics . . . 20 to 50% off . . . DESIGNER FABRIC CLUB, Box 239, Garwood, N.J. 07027

20. Sewing machines, parts and supplies . . . PITTSBURG SEWING CENTER, 511 N. Broadway, Pittsburg, KS 66762.

21. Fashion fabrics at discount, minimum 18 yards per fabric . . . RUCKY D FABRICS 264 W. 40th St., New York, N.Y. 10018

22. WOMEN'S WEAR DAILY 7 E. 12th St., New York, New York 10003 . . . for those in the garment business . . . all kinds of wholesale sources.

23. Another way to save on your telephone bill . . . obtain or use at your library the book on 800 telephone numbers.

24. FABRICS ETC. . . . cotton fabrics . . . send for details . . . 926 Hopmeadow St., Simsbury, CT 06070.

25. SNOOP . . . look at labels, brochures, cartons, anything that you think you could use when you visit other retail stores. Write for info on your stationery and ask for discounts and better prices . . . PERSISTENCE will pay off.

26. AAROVARC, 1191 Bannock St., Box 2449, Livermore, CA 94555 - Embroidery threads, Trims.

27. AMERICAN HANDICRAFTS - Kits, Quilting book, Needlecraft . . . Box 2934, Ft. Worth TX 76113.

28. DICK BLICK (Horton - Box 1267, Galesburg, IL 61401) Fabrics, Dyes, Paints, Trim Book - Craft Art Supplies.

29. BOYCAN'S . . . Box 897, Sharon, PA 16146. Kits/Stencils, Trims, Books-Needle/Craft Supplies.

30. BOYE NEEDLE - 4343 N. Ravenswood, Chicago, IL 60613. Notions, Aids, Quilting Frames, Hoops, Needlecraft Supplies.

31. BUTTON SHOP . . . Box 1065, Oak Park, IL 60304. Sewing zippers, threads, interfacing, buttons, much more.

32. CREATIVE CRAFT HOUSE . . . Box 1386, Santa Barbara, CA 93102. Trims, Books, Craft Supplies.

33. S.R. HARRIS, 5100 N. County Rd. 18, Mn, MN 55428. Full-line notions, threads, fabrics.

34. IMPORTS BY CLOTILDE - 237 S.W. 28th St., Ft. Lauderdale, FL 33315 - Sewing Notions/Aids, Cutting Tools, Quilting Aids.

35. NATURAL FIBER FABRIC CLUB, 521 5th Ave., NY, NY 10125. Sewing Aids, Natural Fabrics, Sewing Aids.

36. SEW CRAFT . . . Box 3293. Marion, IN 46660. Threads, Natesh Rayon, Mexican Rayon, Metallics

NOTES

33

37. TAYLOR'S CUTAWAYS & STUFF, 2802 S. Washington St., Urbana, IL, 61801. Fabrics, Satin Velvet, Cotton . . .

38. LEE WARDS, 1200 St. Charles, Rd., Elgin, IL 60120. Kits: Embroidery, Cross-stitch, Crewel Accessories, Holiday Items.

39. YARN'N SHUTTLE, 199 So. Highland at Poplar. Memphis, TN 38111. Trims/Accessories: belts, shells, feathers, ribbons.

40. ZIPPERS UNLIMITED, 505 McLeod, Ironwood, MI 49938. Zippers: All types.

41. ALLIED FELT GROUP, Division of Central Shippee Inc., P.O. Box 134, Bloomingdale, NJ 07403. Craft Felt.

42. BAZAAR CLOTH, P.O. Box 7281, Santa Cruz, CA 95061. Handwoven all-cotton cloth from Guatemala.

43. BREWER FABRIC SHOP, Twin City Plaza, Brewer, ME 04412. Fabrics, Calicos, solids, Chintz by V.I.P.

44. CAROLINA MILK FACTORY OUTLET, Box V, Hwy. 76, West Branson, MO 65616. Sample Swatches. Fashion designer fabrics.

45. FABRIC OF THE MONTH CLUB, P.O. Box 402098. Miami Beach, FL 33140. Swatches mailed to members. Upholstery offerings.

46. FABRICS, Box 515, Sharon, MA 02067. Fabric assortments ("15 yds. and up wholesale")

NOTES

47. FASHION FABRICS CLUB, 122 Cotter Mill Rd., Great Neck, NY 11022. Swatch folders for member on dress designer close-outs.

48. THE FETTERS CO., 22 West St. Milbury, MA 01527. Felts: Acrylic felt in 24 colors; pieces or put-ups.

49. GRANDMA'S ATTIC, 2055 Alamar, Medford, OR 97501. Hand-printed/screened "country" fabric pieces.

50. LAS MANOS, Box 515 . . . Lower Lake, CA 95457. Handwoven fabric from Guatemala: Contemporary or traditional.

51. LEATHER UNLIMITED CORP., R.R. 1, Box 236, 7155 County Hwy. "B." Belgium, WI 53004. Leathers Incl. garment types.

52. THE MAIL TRAIN, 5401 Dashwood, Suite 2A. Bellaire, TX 77401. "Huckaback" cotton fabric with linen feel.

53. MILL END STORE, 8300 S.E. McLoughlin Blvd., Portland, OR 97202. Fabric - Nylons, Stretch ski pant material.

54. MONTEREY MILLS OUTLET STORE, 1725 E. Delevar Dr., Jamesville, WI 53545. Complete line fur-like fabric.

55. NATURAL FIBER FABRIC CLUB, 521 Fifth Ave., New York, NY 10175. Fabric Club - members get a sewing aids catalog.

56. DAN NEWMAN CO., 57 Lakeview Ave., Clifton, NJ 07011. "Logo" or "Name" cloth.

57. PATTI, 63 Starmond, Clifton, NJ 07013. Fabrics: Callcos, Ginghams, solids; by V.I.P.

58. AUTHUR MURRAY REIN FURS, 32 New York Ave., Freeport, NY 11520

59. VEA PRINTS, 729 Heinz #2, Berkeley, CA 94710. Designs screened on fabric (pieces or patches)

60. UNION RIVER FABRICS, 125 High St., Elks Worth, ME 04605; Designer, imported and other fabrics.

61. CRAZY CROW TRADING POST, Box 314, Dennison, TX 75020. American Indian oriented trims: Beads, Belts, and Ponchos.

62. BUTTON CREATIONS, 26 Meadowbrook Lane, Chalfont, PA 18914. Buttons: Basic and More.

63. DAZIAN'S INC., 40 E-29th St., New York, NY 10016. Boutique/theatrical trims: Spangles, Sequins, Spangle cloths.

64. DISCOUNT CRAFT SUPPLY, 6234 2nd Ave., N., St. Petersburg, FL 33710. Supplies: Beads, felt.

65. DICOUNT LACE CO., P.O. Box 2031, Norwalk, CA 90650. Laces: Eyelet, Polyester, Nylon - variety of sizes.

66. THE EDGE OF LACE - WEST, 4650 S.W. Betts Ave., Beaverton, OR 97005. Trims: Eyelets, ribbons, braids, appliques.

67. ELSIE'S EXQUISIQUES, 205 Elizabeth Dr., Bernen Springs, MI 49103. Trims: Silk, Ribbon, Rosettes, and Rose Buds.

68. THE GREEN HOUSE, Rt. 4, Potsdam, NY 13676. Potpourri mixtures: 12 blends, home grown and collected.

69. GREY OWL/INDIAN CRAFT MFG., 113-15 Springfield Blvd., Queens Village, NY 11429. American Indian oriented trims: Belts, Lacing, Mirrors, Laces, Dried Shells.

70. THE HANDS WORK, P.O. Box 386, Pecos, NM 87552. Handcrafted Porcelain Buttons.

71. HOBBY HUNTING GROUNDS, Box 447, Sedro Wooley, WA 98284. Beads: Bone, Metallic, Sterling, Ceramic, Glass.

71. HOLLYWOOD FANCY FEATHER CO., 512 South Broadway, Los Angeles, CA 90013. Feathers.

NOTES

73. JANYA ASSOCIATES, 49 Longview Rd., Staten Island, NY 10304. Closeouts: May Incl., bead, doll eyes, felt pieces, etc.

74. KEEPSAKE DESIGNS, 571 North Madison, Ogden VT 84409. How-to saving books.

75. KEN'S CRAFT SUPPLY, 250 E. Main St. Midland, MI 48640. Trims: Beads, Pearls, Sequins.

76. KIT KRAFT, Box 1086, Studio City, CA 91604. Beads: Seed, Rocailles, Tile, Others.

77. MAISON MINI, 3647 44th St. Apt. #1, San Diego, CA 92150. Beads (all types - full line)

78. SHERU ENTERPRISES, 49 W. 38th St., New York, NY 10018. Trims: Full line of beads.

79. STREAMLINE INDUSTRIES, INC. 845 Stewart Ave., Garden City, NJ 11530. "Button talk," "Ribbon talk," streamline ribbons; "Colorific" buttons.

80. WOOD FORMS. Foster Hill Rd., Henniker, NH 03242. Wood buttons/beads/

81. FIRST IMPRESSIONS, P.O. Box 682, Fairfield, IA 52556. Graphic rubber stamps "see thru."

82. FLYNNS, Box 985, San Francisco, CA 94101. Fabric cold water dyes in pack or bulk.

83. IVY CRAFTS IMPORTS, 5410 Annapolis Rd., Bladensburg, MD 20710. French colors for fabric painting.

NOTES

84. STENCIL EASE, P.O. Box 225, New Ipswich, NH 03071. Quilt stencil designs.

85. SUSAN BATES, INC., 212 Middlesex Ave., Chester, CT. 06412. Notions/aids.

86. CHILDREN'S CORNER, INC., 4004 Hillsboro, Suite 202, Nashville, TN 37215. Designer patterns: Smocking, French hand sewing.

87. FREDERICK J. FAWCETT, INC., 320 Derby St., Salem, MA 01970. Linen embroidery yarn samples.

88. VIMA, S.P.A., Town and Country Village, 2727 Macrori Ave., Sacramento, CA 95821. Embroidery kits/pattern booklets.

89. THE SMOC BOX, Box 10562. Knoxville, TN 37919. Smocking kits patterns.

90. NICOLETTE BOOREAM, INC., P.O. Box 554, Philmont, NY 1265. Notions, Silk Batting, Patterns.

91. BUNNY PUBLICATIONS, Box 572, Williamsville, NY 14221. "Kissy" Quilt designs.

92. THE COUNTRY COTTAGE, Rt. 1, Box 179. College Grove, TN 37046. Miniature quilt patterns.

93. KIDDIE-KOMFIES, Box 2095, Santa Ana, CA 92707. Kiddie Komfies quilts kits/patterns.

94. MO. P.O. Box 4454. Virginia Beach, VA 23454. Brand name quilting supplies.

95. MARGE MURPHY'S HEIRLOOM QUILTING DESIGNS, 6624 April Bayou, Biloxi, MS, 39532. Quilting and Trapunto designs.

96. QUILT IN A DAY, 3016 Querbrada Circle, Carlsbad, CA 92008. Books.

97. THE TREADLE WORKS, 118 Westridge Dr., Portola Valley, CA 94205. Quilting kits: Amish designs.

98. BRISTLES & NEEDLES, 2724 N.E. 62nd Ave., Portland, OR 97213. Painted fabric designs and patterns/kits for quilted panel vests.

99. CREATIVE EXPRESSIONS, 149 Hazeltine Ave., Jamestown, NY 14701. Sewing how-to booklets on relining.

100. DESIGNER JEANS, INC., 45 E. Gentile St. #2, Layton, UT 84040. Jeans supplies.

These are just a few suggestions that will help you SAVE money when you decide to market your creation. It takes a lot of research and question asking . . . "THE PERSON THAT DIGS THE DEEPEST FINDS THE MOST GOLD."

NOTES

NOTES

CHAPTER SIX

PACKAGING, SHIPPING AND DELIVERING

I stated before that first impressions are important. Your name, price and packaging will tell a lot about your product and your company (which in many cases is just YOU). The product must be protected from the elements and from careless postal and delivery methods. it must also be delivered as fast as possible.

NOTES

A. THE PRODUCT CONTAINER

It could be a plastic garment bag, a paper bag, or an ornate plastic/lucite container.

1. Many times the package will sell the product. If it is attractive, then the consumer will examine it longer.

2. It must convey to the customer exactly what the product is. If the container has to be imprinted by hand or by machine, it should tell what is inside.

3. Make the container see-through or transparent, then it will speak for itself.

4. If possible have the container imprinted with your name, logo and address. This is a great sales tool. That's why groceries, drug stores, etc. ALL have a message on their container . . . the bag.

5. Make sure the container is sturdy enough to protect what is inside. Protection from cold/heat, water, children's sticky hands, etc.

6. If your creation has to be folded or disassembled, then the container has to do all the selling. Be original and make it appealing. Ever see a Hershey Kiss, a L'eggs display box? How about the Kodak yellow package or the Coke red?

7. Try to have a design, color, logo, smell or whatever and carry it through in ALL of your tools of sale.

NOTES

   a) Business card
   b) Stationery
   c) Packaging
   d) Signage
   e) Car — how about Mary Kay and the PINK cars?
   f) Clothes — ever see a Century 21 Gold Sport coat? The McDonald Uniform?

8. You cannot wrap packages with Scotch or masking tape; use strapping tape, cord or metal tape if you are shipping by mail.

B. THE SHIPPING CONTAINER

1. Determine how you can ship your creation, the cheapest and safest way. Talk to your post office and find out the different rates for first, third, fourth etc. class mailings.

2. Ask the post office how heavy, wide and long a shipping package can be.

3. Determine how you can package the product or products so they will not be damaged or opened. There are certain packing materials you can buy that will do a good job without costing a lot. IF YOUR PACKAGE COSTS MORE THAN YOUR CREATION you might have to go back to the drawing board, UNLESS you have another Pet Rock.

4. Make sure you have the logo and message imprinted on the outside of the mailing container.

5. Invest in an inexpensive postal scale. It will save many hours of trips to the post office to have packages weighed.

6. Shipping labels. Investigate the cost of having labels made. You can get 500 peel-off imprinted labels on a holder in rolls for around $25 . . . REMEMBER you want to give the image of professionalism. You want to leave a good impression with your customer. It is important to remember that once a customer has bought from you and accepted your product they will probably buy from you again.

40

7. RECORD all of your customers information, either by filing the original letter or by storing it on a computer. These addresses can be used later for soliciting orders for other products. You can code all the data on the label . . . more on this in the chapter on MAIL ORDER SELLING.

8. If most of your orders are shipped in uniform containers, investigate buying containers in bulk. When I ship books, I put them in Jiffy insulated bags or just plain manilla envelopes. When you buy them in bulk you can save a bundle. Ask your local office supply store for prices and watch your catalogs, compare!

Up to here you have the product made, the price and identifying label, the container and/or the shipping container and the shipping label. You can include:

C. THE SALES MESSAGES/LABEL

1. You may include a history, a story or explanation of the product and/or of your company or yourself.

2. Other products' messages can be inserted. Make sure you have the advertising piece well done. Nothing can turn off a potential buyer faster than poorly done sales material. You probably have many delivered to you each week. Mimiographed, hand written amateurish nothings. Read the chapter on CREATING YOUR SALES MESSAGE.

3. As you advance in your business, consider distribution of other products to supplement yours. These sales messages can also be included in the package. You are shipping the product to the customer for X amount of money and might as well use every advantage. It won't cost any more to include these sales gimmicks. I started publishing and distributing only my books. Then found other great books — so I combined them. See the Example of my first catalog.

NOTES

D. SHIPPING, PACKAGING, SUPPLIES

Listed below are sources for packaging and labeling items that you may need. Write for catalogs; they cost nothing and can give you a lot of ideas. Ideas to make your product more appealing to people with money in their pockets/purses to spend.

Another suggestion: Have your own postcards printed by your "quick printer." Have your own name, which is a marketing tool, imprinted. The 14¢ (as of 1985) post card rate is less than first class letter rate (22¢). Below is an example of my postcards. I leave the back blank. They cost about $7 per hundred.

If an 800 TOLL FREE number is provided — Call and request a catalog — save the postage, always use your business name.

NOTES

STATIONERY SUPPLIES

Stationery supplies, office products

Delmart (1-800-328-9697) 2199 N. Pascal St., Box 64495, St. Paul, MN 55164.

J. William Co., (1-800-241-0854) Box 640, Decatur, GA 30031.

The Business Book, Miles Kimball; (1-800-558-0220)
One W. Eighth St., Oshkosh, WI 54906.

The Stationery House - (1-800-638-3033) 1000 Florida Ave., Hagerstown, MD 21741.

NEBS - (1-800-225-6380) 500 Main St., Groton, MA 01471.

The Drawing Board - (1-800-527-9530) Box 220505, Dallas, TX 75222.

Viking - (1-800-421-1222) 4630 Interstate Dr., Cinn., OH 45246.

Colwell Systems - (1-800-233-7777) 201 Kenyon Rd., Champaign, IL 61820.

Fidelity - (1-800-328-30304) Box 155, Minn., MN 55440

T-SHIRTS, JACKETS SILK SCREENED, IMPRINTED

Primo - 36-25 35th St., Long Island City, N.Y. 11106.

STOCK PACKAGING - Plastic, paper mailing, display boxes
U.S. Box Co. - 1298 McCarter Hwy., Newark, N.J. 07104.

Creative Packaging - 770 Garrison Ave., Bronx, NY 10474.

MINISTICKERS

Bucher Bros. - 729 Leo St., Dayton, OH 45404

MAILROOM SUPPLIES

W.A. Charnstrom - (1-800-328-2962) 9801 James Circle, Minn., MN 55431.

ADVERTISING/PROMOTION ITEMS

Atlas Pen and Pencil - (1-800-327-3232) 3040 N. 29th Ave., Hollywood, FL 33022.

Special Events - (1-800-533-8118) Box 8, St. Charles, MN 55972.

AM PRO - Newton Mfg., Newton, Iowa 50208.

NOTES

43

TROPHIES

Dinn Bros. - (1-800-628-9657) 68 Winter St., Box 111, Holyoke, MA 01041.

FILING/ORGANIZING EQUIPMENT

Magna Visual - 1200 N. Rock Hill, St. Louis, MO 63124.

Jeffco - 205 Hallock Ave., Box V, Middlesex, N.J. 08846.

20th Century Plastics - 3628 Crenshaw, Box 3763, Los Angeles, CA 90051.

American Thermoplastic - (1-800-246-6600) 622 2nd Ave., Pittsburgh, PA 15219.

WRAPPING SUPPLIES (Gift)

Gaylord Specialties 225 Fifth Ave., NY, NY 10010.

Vulcan (1-800-633-4526) Box 29, Vincent, AL 35178.

PLASTIC INDENTIFICATION TAGS

Arthur Blank - 119 Braintree, Boston, MA 02134.

NOTES

E. DELIVERY

How do you get it from you to the customer after it is packaged?

1. The post office . . . you have to take chances on the quality and timing. Some people report excellent service while others would never ship or deliver this way.

2. UPS (United Parcel Service) . . . again it has its ups and downs —More expensive but seems to be more reliable than USP.

3. Express services . . . Federal Express, U.S. Post Office Express, Purolator etc. all will ship your goods or information for a premium price overnight.

4. Independent delivery services . . . there are some excellent local small package delivery services.

5. By bus, airline or rail . . . all will deliver your packages if they travel to the destination you want.

6. By YOU . . . the most reliable and efficient . . . good for local and short distances. It's also good for long distance IF you can make enough profit.

F. MANAGING YOUR INVENTORY

1. EQUIPMENT . . . Take time to record your furniture and machines. In case of theft, fire or disaster, you can prove what you have. A good idea would be to save any purchase slips. I would suggest even taking photos of the more costly items. Example:

ITEM	AMOUNT	PURCHASE DATE	COST	SOURCE
Brother typewriter L10+3	1	11/81	$245	Best
Singer Sewing Machine A3542B	1	11/72	$195	AMA
Olivetti Adding Machine BX-4	1	11/73	$150	Century
Universal Postal scale	1	3/82	$ 85	Halsey
Texas Calculator XL 34	1	5/82	$ 90	Halsey
Commodore Computer	1	6/84	$425	Sears
Commodore Printer	1	9/84	$360	Sears
Office desk and Chair	1	7/79	$500	Halsey
Wastebaskets	2	7/79	$20	Halsey

NOTES

etc. etc.

2. MATERIALS . . . It helps to keep a running inventory of the materials needed to make your creation. example:

Special pattern goods	28 yd.	12/84	$135	ABC
Polyester stuffing	12 pk.	8/84	$ 56	XYZ
Trim assortment	4 rolls	8/84	$ 43	NPQ
Mailing cartons	48	5/84	$ 65	PB Paper
Invoices, PO. etc.	200	3/84	$ 35	Halsey
Imprinted envelopes etc.	200	3/84	$ 28	Quik

CHAPTER SEVEN

PROTECTING WHAT YOU HAVE

If you have a good product and it is well-accepted by the consumer, then the chances that someone will try to steal or copy it are pretty good. You may never prevent all of these possibilities, but you can take basic steps that will discourage and prevent others.

NOTES

A. INSURANCE

Your homeowner's policy will probably be enough to get started IF you are working from your home.
It should cover:

1. Theft of materials or creations

2. Damage from fire, floods, etc.

3. Liability of others on your property.

What it will not cover:

1. Breakage (like sculpturing, porcelain products, ceramics, dolls) . . . I was told by an insurance man that you can get special coverage for this.

2. Product liability . . . Investigate the cost and availability of protection from some KOOK wanting to sue you for an allergy condition or harm that they think your product caused. It might even cause allergies, and you should be insured . . . don't forget insurance sells by the FEAR syndrome. You protect yourself because you are afraid of losing all your money from a lawsuit. Fortunately we can have this protection. Many homeowner's insurance policies will cover you BUT ask your carrier. I have heard of one costing $138/year (Maryland Casualty Company in Baltimore). Much depends on:

NOTES

A. Amount of gross annual sales

B. Number of products in your line

C. Possible risks associated with them

D. Limits to per/ occurrence or per/claim

E. Exposure to children etc.

I won't whip this to death . . . it is worth a phone call to your agency. (See SEWING FOR PROFITS for info on how to pick an insurance agency.)

48

3. Misrepresentation, false claims etc.

4. Workman's Compensation . . . for employees

5. Personal health insurance . . . you may combine other families that are employed by you and have a much lower premium than an individual policy alone.

B. SECURITY

What happens if your creations are stolen? You can get business crime coverage. It covers break-in, hold-up, and mysterious disappearance of monies. It will even cover up a deposit that is on the way to the bank or has been brought home and is stolen.

Of course the best security for your items is common sense and a good lock on your door. IF you have real valuable creations then you must take elaborate steps to prevent someone from taking them. You might have to have an alarm system or even a vault for storing them. If you are displaying at a fair etc., make sure your products have labels, preferably non-removable, (to prevent label switching). If your creations are soilable or breakable then you must display them in showcases or some other way to prevent, handling by greasy fingers or careless children.

NOTES

C. COPYRIGHT, PATENT, TRADEMARK

If you have a unique design that you do not want duplicated, think copyright, patent or trademark. Let's define these and give you some info'.

1. COPYRIGHT LAWS

There are some people who start a business and infringe upon the intellectual property of others, property which is protected by the Copyright Law. Most people do not understand this law and often break it. As a businessperson you must be knowledgeable of this federal law.

To find out more about this law and to quote an expert we called the Federal Information Number (which should be in the front of your phone book) and asked who to call for this information. We talked to Chris Collious of the Copyright Office in Washington.

The copyright law was enacted in 1790 and most recently amended in January, 1978. It is designed to protect the rights of creators of intellectual property in seven broad categories of work:

NOTES

1. literary works
2. musical works, and accompanying words
3. dramatic works, and accompanying music
4. pantomimes and choreographic works
5. pictorial, graphic, and sculptual works
6. motion pictures and other audiovisual works
7. sound recordings

To avoid violating the copyright law, you must learn to recognize and respect all work that is protected by it. A properly copyrighted work of any kind will bear a notice containing these three essential elements:

1. the word "copyright" or its abbreviation, "copr.", or the copyright symbol, ©
2. the year of first publication of the work (when it was first shown or sold to the public)
3. the name of the copyright owner. Sometimes the words, "All Rights Reserved" will also appear, which means that copyright protection has been extended to include all the Western Hemisphere.

Copyright protection for works created after January 1, 1978 lasts for the life of the author or creator plus fifty years after death. If you make a one-of-a-kind item and there are designs or images you wish to protect, be sure to include the proper copyright notice on each item you offer for

50

sale. Your copyright can be conveyed to others only in writing. You may be able to make a Muppet with the approval of the owner and the payment of certain royalties. There are some who have copied E.T., Annie, Raggedy Ann, the Campbell Kids. They are doing this illegally and may open themselves up to litigation.

It does not cost anything to place the copyright symbol and wording on any item, BUT you cannot sue or prevent others from using it without paying the $10 fee and registering with the United States Copyright Office, Library of Congress, Washington, D.C. 20559.

1. Form SE for a serial, periodicals, newspapers, magazines, bulletins, newsletters, annuals, journals, and proceedings of societies.

2. Form TX for nondramatic literary works, including books, directories and other works written in words. This includes How-To instructions for a craft project.

3. Form VA for visual arts, such as graphic, pictorial or sculpural works.

4. Form PA for the performing arts.

5. Form SR for sound recordings.

Send $10 and two copies of the "best edition" of the work.

WHAT CANNOT BE COPYRIGHTED

1. Names, titles, and short phrases (see Trade mark)

2. Inventions (see patents)

3. Ideas

NOTE: The artwork of the Cabbage Patch Kid can be copyrighted. The name can be trademarked and the ingredients or materials can be patented.

NOTES

2. PATENTS

The U.S. government issues a grant giving an inventor the right to exclude others from making, using or selling the invention withing the U.S. It lasts for 17 years and an attorney may cost you from $3,000-$10,000. For information as for the book "General Information Concerning Patents" from Superintendent of Documents, Washington, D.C. 20559.

3. TRADEMARK

This includes any word, name, symbol or device or any combination used by a manufacturer or merchant to identify his goods. Its function is to indicate origin and it serves as a guarantee of quality. You must use your trademark to establish it. It must be used at least once in interstate commerce (between states). Patent and Trademark Office, Superintendent of Documents, Washington, D.C. 20559.

51

D. LAWS AND LICENSES

Included are possible licenses you may need, even if it is a "home business." Some states have "Homework Laws." They may have some effect on your business. It seems that the states of California, Illinois, Pennsylvania, New Jersey and Puerto Rico prohibit toys and dolls from being made at home. These are old laws and unless you have a full-fledged factory I doubt if you will be bothered. It is best to check with you attorney

NOTE: It is important to maintain a low profile (don't shake the neighbor's bush) because:

1. They may turn you in for operating a business.

2. The increased traffic may be annoying to them.

3. The IRS, local tax, and other agencies may start snooping.

4. If it looks good someone else will want to copy

NOTES

County Laws

1. *Occupational licenses. Cities, towns or any other municipality may demand these licenses.*

2. *D/B/A (doing business as) or Fictitious Name Registration Affidavit. To have a legitimate business you have to register with the county. It requires a nominal fee and has to be advertised in a paid advertisement publication three consecutive times (may vary).*

State Laws

1. A state tax number for state sales tax (if applicable).

2. Corporation reports and taxes, usually to the Secretary of State at the state capitol.

Federal Laws

1. IRS. Don't have to say too much about this agency.

2. If you employ others, then all kinds of laws and taxes apply.

3. Small Business Administration (SBA) — agency to apply to for loans.

Regional

1. Better Business Bureau. If you plan on a long-range business it's always beneficial to register with this agency. Many established businesses will agree that BBB does little good for you. It is not possible to use their name in advertising or as a reference. The only time you come in contact with them is if you are doing something wrong, or have upset a customer.

2. Consumer Protection agencies. They may be called by a different name but most counties, cities or states have one. These protect the consumer from fly-by-night and illegal business.

E. USING COMMON SENSE

To protect and keep what you have takes some common sense . . . sometimes this comes from experience and from others who have "paid their dues" by making mistakes. Here are a few suggestions:

1. Don't "brag" about how great business is or how much you are making. There are a lot of envious people out there who would love to steal your ideas.

2. If possible collect all monies yourself. I used to produce seminars on retail crime and security, I found that seven out of ten employees will steal if they are given the chance. My point is, to make sure all monies come to you, "handle it yourself."
Yes, I know some of you are saying that you know that "Joe or Ellen would never take anything from me." Maybe so, but I would like to have a nickel for every "trusted" employee who has stolen from his employer. I would like to have a dollar for every dishonest employee who has caused a business to fail or go bankrupt.

NOTES

3. Do the books (bookkeeping) yourself if possible as you start out. Don't let an employee know too much about your business.

4. Don't assume all customers are honest. Some will steal anything not bolted down. Keep your eyes open.

5. Protect your monies when displaying at a craft fair. When money is involved, there are people who want to take it away from you.

6. Consult with your insurance agent(s) for adequate protection.

7. Mark up your creation enough to pay expenses and make a profit.

8. Don't give away your creation. Charge at least cost unless giving away will initiate review or an order.

NOTES

54

CHAPTER EIGHT
FREE AND LOW COST PROMOTIONS, PUBLICITY AND EXPOSURE

Your should be aware of the high cost to advertise in today's market. Large merchandising companies have highly paid people on their staff who work constantly trying to get exposure for their products. Much of this is free publicity in newspapers, newsletters and magazines. Many times this kind of exposure will do more good than "paid" advertisements. We will review these possibilites:

A. Press release

B. P.R. letter

C. P.R. illustration/photo

D. Testimonials

E. Product reviews in publications

F. Talk shows

G. Newspaper feature sections

H. Writing an article for a national magazine

 I. Displaying your creation in a retail store

J. Donating it as door prize, raffle etc.

K. Offering it free with other products

L. Signage on vehicles etc.

M. Giving away samples to important people

N. Joining organizations and clubs

O. Writing

P. Teaching/Lecturing

Q. Word of mouth

R. Street corner

NOTES

A. THE PRESS RELEASE

Wanna be successful?... THINK BIG! You have a unique product, something that you want the world to know about, something that you KNOW consumers want to buy!! You have already determined that you can produce your creation in sufficient enough quantity to meet *any* expected demand. It will take a little time and effort to create and send out a press release. This is an announcement of your product to others. I have included a sample of releases that I used in the promotion of TEENAGE MONEYMAKING GUIDE and SEWING FOR PROFIT. The principles are the same with any product that you want to promote.

1. WHO do you want the information to go to?

   a. Your previous newspapers and the newspapers in your present area.

   b. Any club, organization, school publication to which you did or do belong.

   c. The appropriate local, state or national publication in your specialty... Quilters to *Quilter Mags*, Woodcarvings to those magazines, newsletters and reports etc.

   d. Throw in a couple of Biggies... *Family Circle, Wall Street Journal* (Yes, there was an article on the front page of the second section about a craftsperson and their unique creation — it made her product a winner.) BH&G, Popular Science. Use your imagination, where would YOU look to find what you create?

2. How do I prepare the information?

   a. You have to make an interesting story. Is it a rags-to-riches story? Is it an original idea, not a copy? Have you made it from unusual materials? Is its use practical and helpful to the general consumer? THESE are the kinds of stories that professional journalists and publications want to print. Stories that will be read, stories that SELL the magazine. The more magazines that are sold, the more companies will want to spend money advertising.

NOTES

   b. You may have a friend, relative, teacher or someone who is good at writing. Enlist their help. Spend a lot of time on your release. I have read hundreds of stories about craftspeople who have had their releases printed in one of the Big Publications and received THOUSANDS of orders. IT IS POSSIBLE!

THE BASIC GUIDE WHEN STARTING YOUR OWN BUSINESS

The public is anxious to buy new and exciting products. Selling them to the consumer can be a costly and complex endeavor. With proper directions, such as outlined in SEWING FOR PROFITS, many talented and creative people can be guided to success. In this book, the reader is gently escorted through the necessary steps to start and operate a business.

SEWING FOR PROFITS has 111 pages created especially for those with the desire to market and sell their creation. Questions such as: Is going into business for you?, Do I have the necessary talent, enthusiasm, resources and preparation?, How do I correctly buy materials and market this creation?, and many more are answered in the 21 chapters.

SEWING FOR PROFIT is authored by Judith and Allan Smith who have been in the sewing, craft and publishing business for over twenty years. They have owned and operated a retail fabric and sewing goods store, conducted sewing classes and seminars and have published newsletters and books.

This 5 1/2 x 8 1/2 softcover edition (ISBN O-931113-01-6) is available from SUCCESS PUBLICATIONS 8084 Nashua Dr. Lake Park, Florida 33410 for $10.00 plus $ 1.00 postage and handling.   —30—

NOTES

Contact: Allan H. Smith
(305) 626-4643

NOW! A GUIDE THAT SHOWS TEENAGERS HOW TO EARN THEIR OWN MONEY

21% of White, 48& of Black and 30% of Hispanic youths actively seeking jobs are unemployed. (Federal Bureau of Labor 1983). The F.B.I. states that 33% of major crimes committed in the U.S. involves unemployed teenagers.

TEENAGE MONEYMAKING GUIDE lists 101 opportunities for youngsters to be their own boss and make money on their own. It includes over 150 illustrations, 50 actual success stories and 12 basic business "secrets."

TEENAGE MONEYMAKING GUIDE clearly outlines step by step procedures:

NOTES

How much it will cost to get started.
Recommendations before starting.
Advice during and after the job.

This No Nonsense guide was researched and written by Allan Smith. He has counseled and taught thousands of young people and has raised five children of his own. This exposure has made him aware of the difficulty teenagers have finding a job.

This 5 1/2 x 8 1/2 softcover edition (ISBN O931113-00-8) is available from Success Publishing, 8084 Nashua Drive, Lake Park, Florida 33410), (305) 626-4643 for $10.00 postage paid.

Satisfaction is guaranteed.

c. What is the correct format? (Study the examples, notice the positioning of the logo and company name.)

1) Note the IMMEDIATE RELEASE and CONTACT name and telephone number.

2) The HEADLINE should be in large type, short in length and give a BENEFIT to the consumer.

3) The BODY should pour on the BENEFITS that the consumer will receive.

4) The next paragraph should tell why the person or company has earned the right to sell, distribute etc., the product.

5) The ENDING should give the particulars of the product and how much it sells for and WHERE it can be obtained. My first press release of TEENAGE MONEYMAKING GUIDE sold hundreds of books . . . SEE how it can be done with little money!

6) End the release with —30—. This means "the end" in publishing language. See Example (1)

7) For a professional job which includes: Letter to Editor, Product Release Letter, Editor Reply Cards & Envelopes, write to Publicity Release Services 616 9th Street, Union City, NJ 07087.

B. THE P.R. LETTER

A lot of times the journalists will print exactly what you send. If it is an interesting NON-COMMERCIAL story. Try to think of a non-commercial message. I am including a P.R. release that I used for SEWING FOR PROFITS. You should use a P.R. letter or brochure on everything you mail out, even to friends . . . possible distributors, wholesalers, exhibit/show producers etc. REMEMBER, you have to CONVINCE others that they want your product. See Example (3)

C. THE P.R. ILLUSTRATION/PHOTO

NOTES

A picture is better than a thousand words. If you can include in your presentation a visual interpretation of your creation, the reviewer or consumer will more likely buy or accept the product. (Notice the Picture of the cover of TEENAGE MONEY MAKING GUIDE).

1. Take a B&W photo against a white or black background.

2. Make sure it is a vivid likeness.

3. Sketch or draw a facsimile.

4. A good photo-copy store with one of those giant Xerox machines can give you a good copy to include in your letter. See Example (3).

5. Notice Example (4). Use the backs of Mailing Envelope for added exposure.

YOU MAY USE ALL THIS INFORMATION FOR DIRECT-MAIL MARKETING IF YOU DECIDE TO SELL VIA THIS ROUTE.

THE **SUCCESS** GROUP

- ADVERTISING
- PUBLISHING
- TRAINING

8084 NASHUA DR. • LAKE PARK, FL 33410

THE BASIC GUIDE WHEN STARTING YOUR OWN BUSINESS

NOTES

80% of American Women sew, and many would like to find a way to sell their creation(s) to the consumer. This can be a costly and frustrating experience.

As editors of craft newsletters, producers of sewing classes and seminars and owners of a fabric/sewing goods store, we were constantly searching for a guide that would help up make the right business decisions. We never did find one so we decided to write one ourselves.

SEWING FOR PROFITS will guide you through the basics of starting out in business. It will show you how to buy materials at the best prices, how to find "start up" money and how to deal with attorneys, accountants and other professionals. It will share information on how to get your family excited about your venture. How to name, price, package, advertise and promote your product and many, many more, useful suggestions.

Reading SEWING FOR PROFITS should be your first step when going into the sewing/craft business. An enclosed order card is enclosed for your convenience. Share in the rewards of selling your products successfully. Enjoy what you do and make money too.

Judy & Allan Smith

EXAMPLE (4)

SEWING FOR PROFITS
JUDY and ALLAN SMITH
8084 NASHUA DRIVE
LAKE PARK, FLORIDA 33410

GUESS WHO READ TEENAGE
MONEYMAKING GUIDE?

ALLAN H. SMITH
8084 NASHUA DRIVE
LAKE PARK, FLORIDA 33410

61

EXPERIENCE THE JOY OF EARNING YOUR OWN MONEY

HERE IS A GREAT GUIDE FOR YOU! If you want to be above average, to stand out as an achiever, to be INDEPENDENT . . . . to be able to buy your own necessities and luxuries in life. TEENAGE MONEYMAKING GUIDE will give you the tools to make it happen! See how others have made fortunes working for themselves. YOU CAN TOO!!!

GUESS WHO THE WINNERS ARE?

YOU DESERVE TO BE A WINNER! The world is made up of WINNERS AND LOSERS. You can be a WINNER by earning money with your own business, by being your own boss. It's not that difficult. . . just read this easy-to-follow guide and GET STARTED.

THESE ARE THE BENEFITS YOU WILL RECEIVE WHEN YOU INVEST $10.00 FOR TEENAGE MONEYMAKING GUIDE:

- 101 possible businesses you can start.
- 12 Basic business SECRETS to be SUCCESSFUL
- How much it will cost to get started.
- Where to find the money to get started
- Recommendations BEFORE you start
- The EASY way to find customers
- "Helpful Hints" to make each job more profitable
- How much you should charge
- How to get referrals and recommendations
- 281 jam packed pages
- 136 illustrations
- 50 actual success stories and MUCH more.

Allan Smith's
TEENAGE MONEYMAKING GUIDE

★ 101 Ways to Start Your Own Business

★ Be Your Own Boss

★ 12 Secrets to Success

HERE IS WHAT SOME OF OUR READERS SAY:

"I made $100 part time in one week by using suggestions in TEENAGE MONEYMAKING GUIDE". David Walsh, Lake Park, Florida

"TEENAGE MONEYMAKING GUIDE is informative and interesting. It should be required reading for ALL young people". Mable Offenheimer, Detroit, MI

"It's a great book. The Twelve Secrets of Business helped me compete and make money." Susan Alongi, Albany, N.Y.

"I grew impatient working for others. TEENAGE MONEYMAKING GUIDE helped me to be my OWN person." Dan Montgomery, Atlanta, GA.

WHAT MAKES THE AUTHOR ALLAN SMITH AN EXPERT? He has been in his own business since the age of twelve. At this age he bought and sold musical instruments. With the profit he bought a set of drums, musical stands, a musical library and started a dance band . . . The bands success earned enough money to put him through college and buy his first car. He has made a fortune being in his own businesses and has taught thousands how they can also make money being in business for themselves.

HERE IS WHAT THE REVIEWS SAY:
This easy-to-read resource can help teenagers of any age to earn money . . "GROUP MAGAZINE"

Sensible suggestions bound to put teenage entrepreneurs on the right track. AMERICAN LIBRARY ASSOCIATION "BOOKLIST REVIEW"

Depending on how closely you take the advice given here, you could even end up being one of those self-made millionaires. "INFORMATION AGE NEWSLETTER."

Headlines: "Book's Moneymaking Tips Help Teenagers Earn Profits." "POST TIMES."

Can't depend on Mom and Dad to supply spending money, buy them a car, buy records etc. TEENAGE MONEY-MAKING GUIDE shows how to earn it on their own. "TOWERS CLUB NEWSLETTER."

YOU WILL ALSO LEARN

- How to know the competition
- Legalities, Licenses, Local Laws
- Low Cost advertising
- How to sell yourself first.
- Selling your business
- Using the telephone to sell.
- Establishing your identity
- Should I hire other people
- Simple bookkeeping
- Door to door selling
- How to create a slinger

Guess Who
Read Allan
Smith's New
Book!

A.   B.

"Figure B" follow the tips and ideas he found in Allan Smith's new book "TEENAGE MONEYMAKERS' GUIDE". As a result, he not only earns enough money to buy his new bike, but he also acquired a new outlook on life, has more self-confidence and a true sense of self-reliance. Characteristics that will help him throughout life!

Hurry! Don't miss this opportunity! "TEENAGE MONEYMAKING GUIDE" will produce extra cash!
Better still it could lead to a full time career!

Send My Copy To _____ ($10.00 plus $1.00 shipping) ($2.00 for First Class)

Name _____

Address _____

State _____
☐ Money Order/Check Enclosed
☐ Master/Visa

Signature _____

Exp. Date _____

Over 250 Pages! Jam Packed With Enough Tips and Ideas to Last a Lifetime!
Remember . . . . 30 Days
Money Back Guarantee!
Order Your Copy Today! Better yet, Right Now!
Could Be The Best Investment You've Ever Made

SATISFACTION GUARANTEED
Your money back if not completely satisfied. (Returned in Saleable condition Postpaid)

NOTES

D. TESTIMONIALS

Nothing beats a good word from a customer. Other potential buyers will be fortified with a "reference" to influence their buying decisions. I have included a sample of the ones I send every time I sell a book. You may get back some negative ones, these are MORE important than the positive . . . WHY? . . . they will point out the things the consumer does not like about your product. Then you can make necessary changes. The rule of thumb is that for every negative comment you get back, there are one hundred more who did not or will not reply AND many more who will not even buy the product. (See the testimonials in example 5)

1. Have a good format and have it typeset.

2. A "quick printer" can produce the amount you need.

3. Send one out or include one with every product sold. This is a wealth of information. Many spend dollars on market research, you can have if for nothing.

4. Pick a few that point out the BENEFIT(s) it gave them. People buy products to SOLVE PROBLEMS.

5. Quote the positive ones in your sales material. Don't use an actual address as they could receive a lot of "junk" mail and will not look favorably on your efforts. Use . . . L. Robbins, Dubouis, PA; D. Miner, N.Palm, Florida, etc. See Example (5).

NOTES

- ADVERTISING
- PUBLISHING
- TRAINING

8084 NASHUA DR. • LAKE PARK, FL 33410

Good Morning:

Thank you for reading TEENAGE MONEYMAKING GUIDE. We hope it has helped you, or will help you soon to make money.

We will be revising this book periodically, both to update its information and to improve its contents. To do so effectively, we need feedback from you, the reader, to improve this book. Could you help us by commenting on both the strength and weaknesses of TEENAGE MONEYMAKING GUIDE. Does it fulfill its purpose? How can we make it better. Has it helped you to make better decisions?

Please use the space below to make your comments and send it to us in the envelope provided.

We will be producing additional promotional material for our national ad campaign: may we use your comments. If so, check below. Thank you.

Sincerely,

SUCCESS PUBLICATIONS

Robin Garretson,
Marketing Manager

NOTES

_____

_____

_____

_____

_____

_____

☐ Check here if we may quote your comments.

Name _____ Date _____

Address _____

Telephone (   ) _____ Occupation _____

65

- ADVERTISING
- PUBLISHING
- TRAINING

8084 NASHUA DR. • LAKE PARK, FL 33410

NOTES

Good Morning;

Thank you for reading SEWING FOR PROFITS. We hope it has helped you — or will help you soon in the sewing business.

We will be revising this book periodically, both to update its information and to improve its contents. To do so effectively, we need feedback from you, the reader, to improve this book. Could you help us by commenting on both the strengths and weaknesses of SEWING FOR PROFITS. Does it fulfill its purpose? How can we make it better. Has it helped you to make better decisions?

Please use the space below to make your comments and send it to us in the envelope provided.

We will be producing additional promotional materials for our national ad campaign; may we use your comments. If so, please check below. Thank you.

Sincerely,
SUCCESS PUBLICATIONS

Robin Garretson,
Marketing Manager

_____

_____

_____

_____

_____

_____

☐ Check here if we may quote your comments.

Name _____ Date _____

Address _____

Telephone ( ) _____ Occupation _____

66

E. PRODUCT REVIEWS IN PUBLICATIONS

This is one of the most influential and impressive types of publicity. I had my TEENAGE MONEYMAKING GUIDE reviewed in BOOKLIST, the American Library Association review publication. This was the turning point for the book. Libraries all over the world sent in orders after seeing it reviewed here. Some suggestions:

1. Find the publication that fits your product. It could be a newsletter, a magazine or newspaper.

2. Find out to WHOM you should send your sample. A lot of times a mail room clerk opens the package, makes his/her judgement, throws it away or takes it home.

3. Ship it by reliable sources.

4. Include:
   a. Press Release
   b. The sample
   c. P.R. letter
   d. Other reviews
   e. An explanation of the product, who made it and the price.
   f. Make sure you include where it can be obtained

5. Follow up in a week or two. Did they receive it, will they consider reviewing it? See my return "review" card example (6).

6. Save all the reviews and put them on one or more pages to use as promotional material. See example (7).

NOTES

67

Example (6)

PLEASE ACKNOWLEDGE

We have Received Your Book _____

We Will Take The Following Action

☐   Your Book Will Be Featured on (date): _____

☐   Your Book Will Be Featured In The Near Future

☐   Please Send More Information _____

_____

_____

SUCCESS ADVERTISING & PUBLISHING
Allan H. Smith, President
8084 Nashua Dr.   Lake Park, FL 33410
(305) 626-4643

NOTES

Name _____

Full Job Title _____

Name Of Publication or Station _____

Mailing Address _____

_____ Zip _____

Comments (Optional) _____

_____

_____

68

REVIEW EXAMPLE #7

Accent

THURSDAY, JULY 19, 1984 — The Post

'...many older people who can't do some of these things (odd jobs). And they don't want these high-priced people who charge $25 an hour.'
— Allan Smith

Book's Moneymaking Tips Help Teens Earn Profits

By Bob Brink

[illegible]

THE INFORMATION AGE MARKETING LETTER™

A RESEARCH & MARKETING TOOL [illegible]

[illegible]

Teenage Moneymaking Guide

THE FREE ENTERPRISE SYSTEM is alive and well -- and it's flourishing, even among the teenage set. We've been in and through that cycle where the parents who had it tough in their own childhood made it too easy for their own offspring by giving them everything and not insisting that they learn to earn their own money. Now the pendulum has swung the other way, and just in time. In the next couple of decades we can look for a more responsible citizenry coming of age and entering the market place or politics. Young people who have learned what it takes to earn their own keep through enterprise and application, will be better businessmen and women and infinitely better legislators. One who is doing something about furthering this movement toward teenage work ethic and responsibility is Allan H. Smith, a Florida pharmacist, author, lecturer for Dale Carnegie Courses, and father of five children. He has just self-published a wonderful book describing 101 ways a teenager can "make" jobs for himself and earn very good money all summer long ... and even during the school year. You'll read more about that book on page six.

HERE'S 101 WAYS TO MAKE EXTRA $

"TEENAGE MONEYMAKING GUIDE" by Allen H. Smith is just about the best self-published soft-cover 6"X9" we've seen in the eleven years we've been looking at 'em! 281-pages and $10.00 is all he's asking, and it's a steal at that price -- because not only will it put your teenager to work making more money than you do, it will put your out-of-work brother-in-law to work also. This is an ingenious collection of entrepreneurial jobs anyone can do in their own neighborhood to earn a good income and stay off the welfare rolls. Depending on how closely you take the good advice given here, you could even end up being one of those self-made millionaires. This is how tycoons get their start. If I were you, I'd order 5 or 10 of these books, and keep them on hand to give as graduation or birthday gifts to every young (and middle-aged) person on your gift list. Order them from us: TOWERS CLUB BOOKSTORE, Dept IAL, PO Box 2038, Vancouver, WA 98668-2038. (Please include 63¢ 4th Class Postage for each book, or $1.50 for First Class Air Mail.)

TOWERS CLUB, USA NEWSLETTER 108
JULY - AUG. 1984 — PAGE FIVE

TCER ALLAN SMITH'S TEENAGE MONEYMAKING GUIDE [illegible]

NOTES

American Library Association "Booklist Review"

Smith, Allan. Allan Smith's teenage moneymaking guide. Success Advertising & Publishing, paper, $10.

Practical advice and an upbeat approach, in both narrative and format, make this useful for junior high would-be entrepreneurs. BE.

Smith, Allan. Allan Smith's teenage moneymaking guide. Illus. by Don Trachsler. 1984. 281p. Success Advertising & Publishing, 8084 Nashua Dr., Lake Park, FL 33410, paper, $10 (0-931113-00-8). CH

Smith is energetic and encouraging in a better-than-average roundup of self-starting business opportunities for ambitious teens. He begins with useful advice on business realities—licensing, self-promotion, insurance, bookkeeping, etc.—following up with job profiles that include estimates of set-up costs, along with a wealth of advice on how to do the job and do it well. Fairly familiar businesses are described—gift wrapping, baby-sitting, cake baking—but the author also suggests a number of innovative ways to turn a profit, among them, conducting home furnishings inventories, lending toys, removing stains from driveways and patios, and extracting tree stumps. While Smith doesn't guarantee success, his business hints are sensible suggestions bound to put teenage entrepreneurs on the right track. Decorated with black-and-white cartoon drawings. No index. Junior high and high school. SZ.

331.34 [OCLC] — Youth—Employment—Self-employed 84-90128

GROUP
OCTOBER 1984

TEENAGE MONEYMAKING GUIDE

ALLAN SMITH

This book conveys the message that teenagers can make money even if they aren't hired by a company. Teenagers can start their own businesses such as car waxing, house sitting, paper routes, snow removal and house painting.

Opportunities for earning money are carefully outlined so you know what to expect before getting started: approximate cost, tools and materials needed, and advertising hints.

The author could have put more emphasis on Christian principles. For example, the book is written so that it betters the "moneymaker," not necessarily the customer.

This easy-to-read resource can help teenagers of any age earn money. Success Advertising and Publishing.

Kelly Averett, 16
Loveland, Colorado

INFORMATION AGE MARKETING LETTER - SEPTEMBER 1984 - VOL. 1 - ISSUE 8 PAGE EIGHT

"TEENAGE MONEYMAKING GUIDE" by Allan Smith is another small but mighty book that will be around for many years, we think. 101 ways for the teenager to make extra money. Ingenious plans that most would never think of on their own. Author is father of five children and saw a need for this information. Spent a full year researching. This is his first self-published book -- and it is done with a masterful hand, from cover to cover. Order your copy today: Book order # 406, ($10.75 ppd). TOWERS CLUB BOOKSTORE, Box 2038, Vancouver, WA 98668-2038. (281 pages, 6" X 9", SC - illustrated, typeset).

F. TALK SHOWS

Every town has a local radio station. Some of the stations are just talk/news. They are constantly searching for interesting subjects to present to their listeners. If you have that story, that unique creation, a rags to riches story, a product that will benefit people, then you have the material they need. If you knit pot holders in one color while watching TV and expect this kind of exposure, the chances are pretty slim . . . BUT if you knit left-handed pot holders and employ handicapped/blind people THEN you have an interesting story.

1. GET YOUR ACT TOGETHER . . . after all, it is an ACT! Have enough products in case listeners want samples or want to buy them.

2. Have a well written P.R. release or introductory letter . . . show this to the program planner (or whoever).

3. Follow through with a phone call. Set up an appointment.

4. Rehearse into a tape recorder with a ficticious

NOTES

talk-show M.C. friend. Have friends critique you on any word-whiskers (Ah's, um's, a's, da's, etc) or imperfections. I don't expect you to be another Paul Harvey, but at least you won't sound like Mortimer Snerd.

5. Have a list of possible questions that the interviewer may ask. You may even hand this to the reviewer to make it easier for both of you.

6. Take a list of purchasers or buyers of your creation AND a group of testimonials (SEE PREVIOUS CHAPTER ON PRESS RELEASES).

7. Take along any positive reviews from periodicals.

8. Be prepared to answer questions . . . What is the next product you will produce, how did you get started, when and where do you work, what do you attribute your success, how does your family accept your work, where did you learn your expertise and talent, do you teach others, where and how much can then be ordered, do you have a patent or copyright, how does someone get a patent or copyright, etc., etc. BE PREPARED!

9. Have someone tape your review. The station might even do it for a small fee.

10. Get a copy of the program schedule with your reviews in it. This is a great P.R. material, just as good as a newspaper article.

11. You may consider a P.O. Box number for the listeners to respond to, you never know about the "kooks" who listen.

12. Send a thank-you letter to the producer and the reviewer. You never know, they may want you back again, especially if you create a lot of listener responses.

13. Source of Radio Stations:
LMP-198? (Literary Market Place), R.R. Bowker, 205 E. 42nd St., NY, NY 10017.

G. NEWSPAPER SPECIAL FEATURE SECTIONS

Closely examine your local newspaper for these.

1. Determine which one "fits" your creation(s).

2. Note the author of article.

3. Send a sample along with ALL support marketing material. Many times a journalist will publish THE letter or P.R. material IF it is non-commercial, objective and interesting.

4. Follow through with phone calls. It may take many to get to the journalists, but keep trying, they may say they never received it so make sure that you address the package to that certain someone, OR better yet, hand deliver.

5. Many times they will send a photographer to your place of work AND interview you over the phone. This will SELL many of your items . . . TRY, TRY AGAIN!!!

6. Try more than one newspaper . . . try to pick the biggies, not the Shoppers Guide or North County Bladder that comes out once a week. You want a paid circulation paper that has credibility.

H. WRITING AN ARTICLE FOR A NATIONAL MAGAZINE

You probably have no idea of the vast number of magazines that are printed, over 10,000 are published — most consumers see only the newstand issues. Your library will have books that list them:

NOTES

1. Find the magazine that fits your creation
   a. Consumer Magazine and Agri-media Dates and Data (SRDS)
      — Standard Rate & Data Service Inc., 3004 Glenview Rd. Wilmette, IL 60091.
   b. Writer's Market Place,
      R.R. Bowker, 295 E. 42nd St., NY, NY 10017

2. Read a few of the articles and get a "FEEL" for the magazine and the writer's style . . . THEN write an article or review. If you have a how-to or rags to riches story, the chances are excellent that they will publish it.

3. Some creators put a small ad to accompany the reviews or article.

4. You may SELL these articles as a series AND these could evolve into a BOOK!

71

I. DISPLAYING YOUR CREATION IN A RETAIL STORE

This is a great way to expose your product to the public.

1. If YOU have a store or a busy office...share-display. You show their product and they show your product.
2. If the item is fragile or soilable, enclose it in some kind of protective device. They sell Doll-bubbles, plastic clothes bags, small display cases, plastic coatings etc.

3. Have a descriptive sign or brochures available for the viewer to pick up, examine and take home.

4. Have a way the examiner can order, either through the displaying store, via mail, or at yor place of business.

5. If you don't share-display, then have an agreement with the cooperative store-owner, a share of the profits, a rental fee or a favor.

NOTES

6. Like consignments, make sure you have an agreement that states who is responsible if it is damaged, stolen or missing. Check with your insurance and theirs and find out what is acceptable.

7. Pick a store that is compatible with your creation. Don't put a doll at a corner gas station, or a set of home-forged, hand-carved handle hunting knives in a women's dress boutique. (I have a friend from Clewiston, Florida, in the middle of the state, who has hand-made such knives. He can't make them fast enough. They are of high quality, and he sells most of them through a display in a local hardware store.)

ANOTHER NO-COST METHOD OF MARKETING AND EXPOSING YOUR CREATION

J. DONATE IT AS A DOOR-PRIZE, T.V. PUBLIC AUCTION OR RAFFLE ITEM

A great way to get FREE exposure and public awareness.

1. Many organizations are continually looking for door prizes. If you donate one, make sure you get the maximum publicity.

2. Find a public TV station. They are always looking for goods to auction off. If yours is an exciting item it will cause a lot of interest and bidding.

3. Organizations look for items to raffle. They may even PAY you for one or more.

4. Donate one or more to charitable or not-for-profit organizations to raffle.

5. Make sure your creation is clearly marked (with non-removable labels for marking) and with advertising or promotional material attached.

6. Use this as a P.R. item . . . "ABC creations has just donated 35 wood-carved figures to the ANY TOWN orphanage to use in their annual fund raising auction."

K. OFFERING IT FREE WITH OTHER PRODUCTS

Find another similar or opposite product and offer to sell it at a discount to offer in combination or as a free bonus with their item. You've seen lighters given away FREE with a cartons of cigarettes, shoe polish FREE with the purchase of a pair of shoes, etc. BE IMAGINATIVE AND CREATIVE, think of what you would like as a customer and tailor-make your own deal. If the other product is well-accepted you may ride its coat tails and find a lot of exposure this way. If you are starting a newsletter, arrange to give it away with the local newspaper or a certain magazine.

L. SIGNAGE ON VEHICLES ETC.

You should advertise your item on the side of your car, on the license plate, on every piece of mail you send out. (See example of the way I use my envelopes). Here are a few more suggestions:

1. Hand paint or have imprinted balloons to give away.

2. Put calling cards or notices on bulletin boards.

3. Have bumper stickers for your friends' and relatives' cars.

4. Paste stickers on places that will allow announcing your creations.

5. Hand imprint t-shirts, shirts, jackets etc. with your message. The owners of BULL FROG sun screen did exactly this: they even gave away small one-dose samples. They became very successful using some of these low cost P.R. gimmicks.

6. Put signage on all vehicles, bikes, mopeds, snow-mobiles, baby carriages, etc. MANY WORRY ABOUT "WHAT WILL THEY THINK IF THEY SEE THESE GIMMICKS" . . . Who Cares, you want to be successful or create an image that you think others want you to be.

M. GIVING AWAY SAMPLES TO IMPORTANT PEOPLE

Those who can give you a free plug or publicity. It's done more than you think. Send one to columnists, journalists, newscasters, TV announcers, anyone whom you think could give you some free publicity. Don't be obnoxious and call every day. "Remember that hand-made Christmas wreath I sent you last week? Have you mentioned

NOTES

73

it on your TV show yet?" A good way is to include a cordial letter saying that you are sending this "out of appreciation for the good work you have done for crafters in the past. Please accept this as our appreciation."

N. JOINING ORGANIZATIONS & CLUBS

This exposure will benefit you in many ways:

1. You will learn what others do, grasp on to the positive feedback.

2. Softly let it be known of your creation/product.

3. Volunteer to become involved . . . again you will be the winner.

4. Be willing to donate your product for a door-prize, raffle, etc.

5. A good way to look for potential employees and investors,

6. A good way to find the BEST bankers, insurance agency, accountant, attorney, merchant, etc.

7. A source of names for mailings, home-shows, etc.

NOTES

8. Offer to speak, lecture or hold a seminar on your expertise. I joined Chamber of Commerce and held a series of seminars on various topics on which I was an expert. It gave me great exposure.

9. Don't be obnoxious and overdo the selling. We all have had over-enthusiastic Amway/Shaklee and insurance people bore us to death. I had one of them in my "How to start a Home-Based Business" class at the college. He could not objectively converse without injecting (BLEEP) company and it's philosophy. He soon was ignored and did a lot of harm for the company's image. I don't want to underestimate these companies' successes, nor the enthusiasm of their sales forces, just want to make a point.

10. Don't join just to be a name on the membership roster. If you do, spend your time on something else. You only get out of an organization what you put into it. Its much like marriage, religion, school, friendships and family.

74

O. WRITING

There are many successful people who have either used writing to promote their creations OR have written because of a successful product. The public likes to learn HOW TO DO IT. If you can relate or communicate by writing a story or a set of instructions, then you can capitalize on this also.

1. After writing four books, I found many short-cuts and errors. So I started a working manual for myself for the next book. I decided to pursue my Doctorate in Management which entails the writing of a Dissertation. Yep! You guessed it, it was on HOW TO SELF PUBLISH AND SELL YOUR BOOK. I now want to put together a writing seminar.

2. Judy, my wife, loved and collected dolls for a great period of her life. She gathered information and put together a source and supply catalog, formed a Doll Club, organized a workshop and wrote a newsletter.

3. Clotilde Yurich Lampe was a sewer, a workshop teacher. She started selling sewing goods via the mail and became such an expert that she gives 200 lectures a year throughout the country.

4. Barbara Brabec a craftsperson most of her life, started a newsletter SHARING BARBARA'S MAIL, wrote and published CREATIVE CASH and HOMEMADE MONEY, books then enlarged her newsletter to a semi-magazine NATIONAL HOME BUSINESS REPORT.

5. Jerry Buchanan started writing and placing classified ads in newspapers for his books. He then started a club/newsletter for writers called TOWERS CLUB, then started another newsletter, INFORMATION AGE

6. Margaret Boyd, another successful sewer wrote two national selling books, CATALOG SOURCE FOR CREATIVE PEOPLE and THE SEW AND SAVE SOURCE BOOK.

7. Dan Poynter loved to spend time parachuting and hang gliding. He decided to write books on the subjects and became very successful as a publisher and author.

NOTES

DIFFERENT AREAS OF WRITING:

1. A Press Release
2. A review article to send in with the creation
3. An article for a specific publication
4. Book(s)
5. A lecture
6. A class or course
7. A manual for training

WRITING (cont)

A lot of you are thinking that you could never put together an article that would teach others AND be interesting. POPPY COCK! You may get to enjoy it:

1. The best way to get started is to find a periodical (newspaper, newsletter, magazine) that fits into your kind of craft/hobby/skill.

2. Read a few of these and feel the style of the authors of articles. Study the advertisement . . . soon you will grasp the "personality" of the periodical.

3. Next determine what you are an expert on. To be able to relate to others and make it interesting you should know ten times more than what you are writing. Choose a subject that you think the majority will want to read.

4. Make an outline of your thoughts then write the article.

5. Send it to only ONE magazine at a time.

6. Address it to the editor or publisher by name.

7. Wait . . . and start on another article.

8. Be prepared to receive rejects UNTIL you finally have one accepted, talk about P.R.? These articles are better than reviews. You will get numerous letters and inquiries.

9. Many book authors start this way by combining the articles into a book.

NOTES

P. TEACHING/LECTURING

High school and college adult education schools are BEGGING for people to teach practical courses for adults, courses that would motivate them to attend. Call your local high school/college and inquire. This is a great ego-booster and will get your thoughts organized. It will help you in your hobby/craft also. A good teacher/lecturer should learn more than the students she/he is teaching. This kind of exposure is great for your products. You can share them with any class members and receive any feedback that will be constructive. You may even SELL some. I will sell my workbook for $35 in my WRITING seminars. Clotilde sell 65% of her class members her book SEW SMART.
ATTEND SEMINARS, WORKSHOPS AND LECTURES. Before you do, consider these questions!

1. Is it the best use of my time?

2. Will the program be specific to a problem of opportunity?

3. What is the experience level of the attendees?

4. Is the instructor knowledgeable and will I learn anything?

5. Is there an opportunity for exchange of information?

6. Can I do any follow-up to promote, sell or improve my product?

7. Can I learn anything by making friends in the class?

I must have hundreds of examples of classes conducted for small business, home-based business, craft business info, etc. Community and junior colleges are offering courses tailored to small businesses more and more. There are places to go for help in rural areas as well. U.S. SBA, district offices will often set up shop in rural communities, The area Chambers of Commerce may form economic development groups and workshops.

The more exposure you have, the more knowledge others will have about you and your product.

WHERE CAN I LECTURE OR TEACH:

1. To your family, if they will listen

2. To local schools. Social Sciences etc. classes always welcome parents that can talk about success for careers to students.

3. Organizations, clubs

4. Peer groups and clubs

5. Seminars that you charge to "show how."

6. As a paid public speaker on a speaking tour.

NOTES

77

Q. WORD OF MOUTH

This is probably the most effective and lowest cost of any kind of publicity. You, your product's and your businesses reputation is at stake. How many times have you had bad experiences with either rude clerks, don't care management or unreliable merchants? All of us have a "circle of influence" of about 200 people. Our family, friends, merchants, professionals, church, organizational, etc. . . . people that we come in contact with. Notice that reputations can be mentioned to quite a few people (either positive, or negatively.) Many businesses get their customers by word of mouth. Consumers like to share their experiences with others. They want others to shop or buy where they have. It gives them a sense of doing something that someone else has not. It also gets their friends to do the same thing they did, thus creating a common interest. You have to treat everyone with respect and courtesy . . . if not, the word will soon spread. I have seen many superior services and products fail because of the attitudes of the owners and or their employees.

NOTES

R. STREET CORNER

Don't laugh, many companies have got into street promoting. It is the best way to develop quick public awareness for promoting a new product or service.

1. It is best just to introduce NOT SELL . . . slingers, pictures, descriptive literature, etc.

2. The boothe must SCREAM at pedestrians. Use bright colors or even balloons. Hire attractive people dressed in some kind of clothing that makes them stand out . . . special hats, shirts, vests, etc. Use a brightly colored sign.

3. If you are not selling anything there are usually no legal problems. A vendor's license isn't required because money never changes hands. The sidewalk booth is only for demonstrating a product or service.

4. The only drawback is that it is short-lived.

5. The best place is in the heart of the city, where people with the most discretionary income are likely to walk by. Stay away from shopping centers. Most of the people there are browsers.

CHAPTER NINE

SELLING YOUR PRODUCT

Now let's continue other ways to sell or expose your creation

A. What is marketing?

B. How to sell

C. Advertising

D. Signage

E. Marketing areas (30 possibilities)

F. Who can I sell to? (100 possibilities)

NOTES

79

A. WHAT IS MARKETING

Fifty years ago, a Boston millionaire unintentionally sentenced his heirs to poverty by stipulating that his entire estate be invested exclusively in electric streetcar utilities.

Like the electric streetcar business, every major company was once a growth company. But where growth slowed or stopped, it did so not because the market became saturated, but because there was some lack of management foresight.

- The *railroads* are in trouble because they limited their business to the rails rather than "transportation," ignoring a need for expanded freight haulage by truck and air.

- *Hollywood* barely escaped total devastaion from television; it thought it was in the movie business rather than entertainment.

- *Dry cleaning,* a growth industry in an age of wool garments, now faces decline because of synthetic fibers.

NOTES

- The *corner grocery store,* well established in the 1930s, never recovered from the competition of the supermarket.

- *Electric utilities* are supposedly a "no-substitute" industry. Yet solar energy and chemical fuel cells may spell their end.

In each case, the industry's strength lay in the apparently unchallenged superiority of its product; it was a runaway substitute for the product it replaced.

MARKETING is the most important function of selling a product. It is the difference in failure and success of doing business. MARKET RESEARCH . . . sounds kinda' big business, not really . . . you must do a couple of things to determine if your creation is going to be bought.

1. How large is the potential market area — two blocks, city-wide, state-wide, national, world wide?

2. How much money can you make in what period of time?

3. What share of the market can you take with your product?

4. Where are my potential customers located — in the home, office, jails or beaches?

5. What type of person will buy my product and WHY? REMEMBER AN IMPORTANT FACT . . . PEOPLE DON'T BUY PRODUCTS, THEY BUY SOLUTIONS TO PROBLEMS . . . in your case, maybe a need for something soft and cuddly, something to make them smile and forget their problems.

6. What price is the competition, if you have any?

7. What MEDIA should I use to promote the product — direct mail, radio, TV, door to door, etc.?

BASIC OVERVIEW OF MARKET RESEARCH

Product life cycle isn't just some isolated and abstract business concept. Customer buying patterns are just the primary determinants of the product life cycle. Thus the life cycle helps you to keep in touch with your market — the people "out there" who pay real cash for your product. But life cycle is only a reflection of market conditions. Essential market information comes from market research.

What is market research?

Market research is a methodical search for a comprehensive, accurate, and useful description of your market. It should help you to answer any of the following questions:

1. *Market Potential and Characteristics. How large* is the estimated market in terms of units and dollars? What *growth rate* can be expected? What are the *potential profits* in the market? What *share of the market* can be expected? *Where* are the potential customers located (the work force, geography, etc.)?

2. *Consumer Attitudes and Needs. Who* will buy this product? *Why?* What are the main perceived advantages and disadvantages of the product? *How often* will the product be bought?

3. *Price Information. At what price* are *competitive* products being offered? At what *price* should *our* product be sold?

4. *Product Information.* What are the prime *characteristics* of *competitive* products? *How* will our product be *perceived* by the consumer?

5. *Promotion.* What *media* should be used to help sell the product (i.e., radio, TV, print, etc.)? *What points* should be *stressed* that will be most effective in selling the product?

6. *Place* (channels of distribution). What *distribution channels* should be used to sell the product? *How* can the product be *moved* most efficiently from the producer to the consumer?

NOTES

You may not need the answers to all of these questions, so be clear about what you *do* want before the research gets underway. You save time and money by knowing what you want before you go after it.

I have taught numerous classes and advised many others about selling their product(s). MOST people go into business with very little preparation. Many will not even take the basic advice and prepare for the problems and hurdles they may come across. The more prepared you are, the more likely you will be successful and make money. Every minute you spend researching and finding answers to questions BEFORE you start, the more hours you will save AFTER you begin.

I have written many books. The first three were total disasters, I must have made every mistake imaginable. I did not prepare or examine any other's suggestions, I blindly wrote the text and had it printed. I soon found my errors in not preparing. The next two books were fairly successful and the others very successful. I had learned from MY MISTAKES, not the mistakes of others. I became so incensed with these bloopers, that I wrote a comprehensive manual . . . HOW TO SELF PUBLISH AND SELL YOUR OWN BOOK.

NOTES

B. HOW TO SELL

Many people hate to sell. Just to mention the word stirs up all sorts of negative images — the pushy salesperson, people bending the truth, inferior products with high prices, undelivered books. But as a craftsperson, selling is an essential part of the business. If craftspersons don't sell, they don't eat and don't continue to do what they like best, making crafts. Selling is something we all have to do. You Must!

1. BELIEVE IN YOURSELF!

2. BELIEVE IN YOUR PRODUCT!

3. BELIEVE THE PUBLIC WILL BUY!

4. BELIEVE THAT YOU HAVE TO MAKE A PROFIT!

5. BELIEVE YOU CAN SELL!

This is not a lecture on Selling BUT let's review some basics that may help you SELL your creation to the public, wholesalers, reviewers or whomever.

1. You have to SELL yourself first.

2. Dress, act, talk and show respect professionally when making any kind of presentation.

3. Make appointments, verify them and be on time.

4. It is tough to continuously do business or be in business with friends and/or relatives (there are exceptions).

5. Tell the truth.

6. Follow through on ALL promises.

7. NEVER talk down competition.

8. ASK for the money or the order.

9. Assume you are, and you are, just as good as any other salesperson.

10. Stick to your price list, and you must have one. Don't make "side deals." They come back to haunt you later.

11. Try to collect up-front or C.O.D. (with dealers) . . . the least amount of paper-work the more profit you'll make.

12. Have all sales material professionally done. A real "turn-off" is to have Xeroxed or mimeographed receipts etc.

13. Always maintain the SUCCESS ATTITUDE . . . keep thinking "I will make this sale, I will be successful!" And you will be.

14. Be trustful but wary. Don't trust everyone.

NOTES

83

C. ADVERTISING

There are many types of advertising. You have to decide on a plan and a budget (how much of your monies you will spend on advertising). Refer to the chapter on FREE AND LOW COST P.R. for advertising possibilities. If you want to place an ad in a magazine or other print, here are some money making suggestions:

1. FORM AN ADVERTISING COMPANY . . . sound complicated?, not really.

a. Think of a name different from your own.

b. Register it with the proper authorities . Have a d/b/a/ or fictitious name registered. This will give you authenticity with the potential advertising media.

c. Learn the language.

   1. R & D . . . rate and data . . . the rates, publication dates the magazines etc. have.

   2. P. O. Purchase order number . . . some use this for every transaction

   3. MEDIA . . . whom you are advertising with and what specific issue, section, page etc.

NOTES

   4. INSERTION DATE . . . what issue it will be place in.

   5. E.O.M. . . . end of the month. Some will give a 2% discount if paid 2% 10/E.O.M.. You deduct 2% from the total amount owed if paid by the tenth of the following month.

   6. AGENCY . . . a recognized advertising agency.

   7. CAMERA READY . . . your ad must be ready for publication to insert without doing any art or type work.

   8. 3 X's DISCOUNT . . . usually a 5% discount if the ad is run, unchanged, three consecutive times.

d. Have stationery, envelopes and order forms printed. Use them every time you correspond with the media. (see example.)

e. Don't use a post office box if possible. Many people think you are trying to "hide" something or are not legitimate.

f. Have a separate bank account for the advertising company.

g. Use the bank account every time you pay for any advertising materials.

h. If possible have a business phone that can be listed in the yellow pages. You'd be surprised that many companies think this is the mark of authenticity. They will check to see if you are listed, yes, even if they are from out of town.

i. Have other business use your advertising company if possible —anything to build your reputation so you can save dollars.

SUCCESS ADVERTISING CO.
8084 NASHUA DRIVE • SUITE 301
LAKE PARK, FLORIDA 33410

ORDER NUMBER _____

PLACED BY _____

DATE

CLIENT

PRODUCT

MEDIA

INSERTION DATE

AD

THE SUCCESS GROUP
PUBLISHING • ADVERTISING • TRAINING

ALLAN SMITH
PRESIDENT

8084 NASHUA DRIVE
LAKE PARK, FL 33410

SPECIAL INSTRUCTIONS

RATE

SIZE OF AD

85

COST _____

LESS AGENCY DISCOUNT _____

LESS CASH DISCOUNT _____

NET AMOUNT _____

EXAMPLE OF ADVERTISING STATIONERY

j. Realize that you will have to pre-pay for the ads until you build up credit. You may have to fill out financial forms for some companies.

k. You may have to pre-pay months in advance as many publications solicit ads three to six months ahead of time.

l. If you pick a certain media to advertise in, try to find out the head person and talk to him personally. He/she can do a lot of favors. I once advertised in a leading Woman's magazine and learned from the advertising director that a free listing was available. I "pulled" more interest from this listing than from the ad. As a writer of books, I also had an "inside" to the editor who may "review" my books.

m. Don't ever take advantage of those you deal with. They will gladly give you this 15% discount if you are an established agency.

n. Classified ads do not earn the 15% discount.

o. Many experts say that mail orders under $20 will not generate a profit.

p. Experts also say that you must run an ad three times to have a success or failure decision.

q. Don't start with a large ad. Test with a classified ad first, then grow to large ones.

2. CREATING THE AD

a. The ad must bring in enough money to pay for the creation of the product and the ad money.

b. Classified ads . . . experts say these ads are good for building up mailing lists. You cannot ask $12.50 for imprinted aprons outright. You can ask for responses to "a free offering" or information.

c. It is always best to charge a nominal amount for the catalog information or sample. Make it an even dollar ($1, $2) as many will send the actual cash

NOTES

d. Insist on U.S. FUNDS. Many from Canada and other countries buy American magazines. They will have to pay in U.S. funds or you will be out money if their currency is of lower value.

e. Do not send your materials C.O.D. If you get stuck with a no-show, you will have to pay for charges both ways.

f. Accept checks.

g. State "Money back" guarantee. It can increase responses 20-30%.

h. Accept Master/Visa . . . this can increase responses 20-30%. You will have to contact a bank that will deal with mail order companies. I would advise you not to highlight your mail order business. Many of you probably derive most of your revenues from other sources. Stress these other sources. You should have credit approval before you ship your Master/Visa orders.

i. TEST! TEST! TEST! Use small ads first. Use smaller ad inserts in different periodicals. You can waste a lot of monies advertising IF you don't know the basics.

j. Ask experts How To create an ad.

k. Don't cover every inch of space. Leave some "white space" for the eye to focus on the important aspects or wording in your ad.

l. Do some research. Read a book on creative advertising. Notice what ads are repeated on similar products as yours.

m. Realize that many companies do 100% of their business by ads and mail order . . . you also can if you create an interesting ad to which the consumer will respond.

3. EVALUATING THE RESULTS:

a. The cost of advertising is part of the cost of the product.

b. If an ad is pulling well, DON'T CHANGE IT!

c. You can test different prices with different ads in different periodicals.

d. Code your ads. Each should have a way for you to know where the response came from. Change the spelling of the address slightly, put a letter after your address (i.e. 8084A Nashua would mean it came from an ad in *Family Circle* . . . 8084B would be a *Craft Woman* ad etc.)

e. TRACKING CHART . . . Formulate a Tracking Chart. This will keep track of the responses you receive from the ads. (see example)

f. Don't "beat a dead horse." If the ad is a dog, change it or forget the publication and go to others.

g. Don't exceed the budget amount you have designated for advertising.

D. SIGNAGE

1. If you are in a rural area, you may put an identifying sign on your garage, barn, chicken coop, etc. Ever see a Mail Pouch sign? In our travels throughout the U.S. Judy and I have noticed many signs advertising all kinds of homemade creations on homes, fences, Hay wagons, snowmobiles, tractors, etc.

2. As a bumper sticker - when the Doll Society was active we had I LOVE DOLLS bumper sticker made up.

3. As a T-shirt — Grandma's Home Made Chocolate Chip Cookies, etc.

4. As a lapel button that friends, relatives and family can wear.

5. Slingers, brochures, pamphlets to leave around.

6. On cars, trucks, wagons, mopeds, submarines, etc.

7. Rent space on billboards, semi-trucks, other people's vehicles.

8. Hot air balloons, kits, regular helium-filled balloons to give away with your messages on it.

9. On bowling alley score sheets.

10. Sunday Press in Lake Worth, Florida sells space in church bulletins nationally. George Blumel sells the ideas to churches so that they can underwrite the cost of printing and distributing the bulletin by selling ads. He gets the ads, prints and sends the church a check for their portion of the revenues . . . What an idea!

11. In buses, rapid transit, trains, subways — space is available.

12. On city, town, public benches.

13. On the plastics covers of waiting room magazines.

15. On Dog Sweaters

Use Your Imagination and Ingenuity!

NOTES

87

E. MARKETING AREAS.

Listed are 29 areas of marketing. Marketing simply means ways to get someone to notice or buy your product. You will have to examine these areas and decide which will fit your budget. (YOU MUST HAVE A PROJECTED BUDGET.) Which one will be the most effective for you and your product? Which one can be done efficiently and profitably? This choice could make or break you. Very few home creators can afford to be in more than one or two market areas. Decide which is best for you and go for it. If it doesn't work out after a specific amount of time and money is spent, switch to another. Remember that PERSISTENCE pays off. Some people give up too soon. Did you ever read Acres of Diamonds? It tells about a person who constantly looked outside his home for his fortune and found out later that it was right where he was. He needed faith in himself and persistance . . . If you feel strongly about a certain marketing method, then search out other books, newsletters, courses and individuals that will teach MORE. Let's review the essential that you should have BEFORE you decide on a marketing plan:

1. The amount of money that you can spend . . . BUDGET.
2. The time you have to spend on this area.
3. The amount of knowledge and information needed.
4. If it is suitable for your kind of product.
5. Can you test this area before spending a lot of money?
6. What are the average return rates on which you can measure your efforts? (i.e. The average rate of return for a mail order effort asking for money is 1 to 1½%.)

NOTES

1. CRAFT SHOWS

I mention this first because it is a good way to start, to test your creation. You may find craft shows in many locations and sponsored by a variety of groups: Elks, Masons, churches, temples, schools, city halls, Hell's Angels, Moonies, Women's Club, whatever. Find the group with which you will be comfortable, and one where your goods will be accepted. Swastikas at St. Gerards and Bibles at a motocycle parts show may both "Bomb."

Here is a great way to get attention and sales for your product or creation. The originator of the Cabbage Patch Kids peddled his creations from fair to fair for years before they became a national sensation. The Hula Hoop was started the same way at local county fairs. Here are some suggestions and facts that may help you make a decision about renting that table, booth or space:

1. Realize that you must have an eye-appealing display. You have to get the attendee to STOP at your place to look and to BUY.

2. Have enough stock to satisfy the demands to buy your creation.

3. Be attentive when you are there. A turnoff to the public is to have a bored disinterested person at the table or booth reading a book.

4. Bring refreshments and things to keep you busy. You may sit for hours without talking or seeing anyone. Then again you may be so busy you won't have time for that cup of coffee. If you are alone, find someone who can relieve you when you go to the washroom. Drink very few liquids. Presidents, kings and queens have to limit their intake of liquids before appearing at some function. Because of security reasons a queen can't just say, "Would anyone like to join me? I have to go to the Ladies Room."

5. Have a brochure/slinger and calling cards to give to interested people.

6. Have a note book to record suggestions people make or that you notice. Also for follow-up sales calls.

7. If possible have a Master/Visa card account. Your local banker can advise you on this. **This can increase sales up to 30%.**

8. Always get at least a 50% deposit on special orders that people request.

9. If it is cold have enough clothing. If in the sun and heat have a shade and appropriate clothing.

10. Keep your eyes open. Unfortunately there are some who may want to steal your goods. Keep your money out of sight. If it gets to be a large amount have it secured or taken away.

NOTES

11. Make friends with displayers on each side of you. You can watch out for each other and spend "slow times" chatting.

12. Wear a uniform or shirt that advertises your creation. There are many t-shirt stores that can make up one for you. You are a sewing professional; you should make an apron, hat, etc., to make you stand out.

13. Have a price list and stick to it UNLESS you are prepared to haggle over prices. In some countries in the world this is the custom, to play the price game.

14. If you want to participate in a large county or state fair, you must make plans about six months ahead of time. You must reserve a space, send in a deposit and make plans.

15. Start with a small craft show first, analyze your successes, then make the decision whether or not to move to a larger affair.

16. Make an effort to find out how many people are expected (from past shows' attendance) and have enough handouts, etc.

17. If you are doing the show with friends or family set up a work schedule, write it out and beforehand and make it CLEAR to everyone involved.

18. Find out what is furnished. Do they have tables and chairs, etc? Here is a check list that may help you:

NOTES

Date of show	Parking
Places of show	Security during show
Times open	Security when closed
What is provided	Lighting
Electrical outlets	Heat/cooling
Restrooms	Water
Set-up times	Refreshments
Close-up/packing time	Pre and post set-up times
Approximate attendance	Deposit
Size of booth/display area	Cancellation fees
Cost of booth/display area	Wrapping materials (bags, etc.)
Person in charge	Change (silver/dollars)
Sales slips	Tax records
Local ordinances	

19. Is what you are selling enough to cover your show expenses?

20. Does your price list reflect quantity discounts and wholesale prices?

21. Take a beginning inventory and an ending inventory. Compare it with the sales slips. This way you can determine what was stolen or not recorded.

22. Research the price you put on your creations. Is it too high or too low? Compare with similar items that others sell.

23. Determine if you are going to let the public "dicker" with prices. We recommend not doing this. You have worked hard to make your creation; stick to the original price. If you want to "close-out" an item THEN discount it.

24. Make sure EVERYTHING is marked and preferably with labels or stickers that cannot be removed or switched.

25. Have a procedure for customers or special orders. Either get full price up front or a 50% deposit.

26. Have a sign-in book AND get the addresses of all your customers. You can use these for direct mail sales. We have seen some sharp exhibitors run a FREE DRAWING. They collect hundreds of addresses that way. You can give away one of your creations and use the addresses to send sales information later.

27. An idea for a change box is to use a fishing tackle box. (Make sure you take enough change)

28. Decide if you will accept personal checks or not. We suggest you accept them.

29. You will be asked to give senior citizens discounts. Make that decision and put it on your price list.

30. Check out sources for bags and wrapping materials.

31. If a demonstration will help your product GO FOR IT! Did you ever see the way glass blowers or pottery makers stop traffic? You could take along your sewing machine. This would keep you busy during slack times, help to produce more products and be a show stopper. Many others would feel they had a common interest with the machine and will stop, shop or talk.

32. Make sure you have any required licenses and tax numbers. Check ahead, some localities have strange laws.

33. Can you secure your goods at night? Or do you have to take them down, pack them up and bring them back the next day?

34. If you have come from another area, have you made plans to stay overnight?

35. Does your display protect your items from the hands of small children? They are naturally going to handle your goods.

NOTES

36. One of the best ways to stop a potential customer is to WEAR A SMILE and give a cheery greeting.

2. FLEA MARKETS

A lot of people get their start at a flea market. Probably because it is low cost and easy to set up. Here are a few thoughts on the matter:

1. Most items are low cost or second hand. This makes it hard to sell a quality craft/sewing item.

2. If your product can be made in a large volume and for a moderate cost you might have a chance. We have visited dozens of these markets and they run from "junk groups," to some pretty good vendors. The higher quality shows should be classified as "craft shows."

3. Visit as many flea markets as you can BEFORE making a commitment. You can feel the difference. Many are held at drive-in theaters and parking lots. The outdoor ones are usually of lower quality. Then there are the permanent flea markets. There is one in Lake Worth, Florida that has been in existence for about 50 years. Many participants have been there for a long time.
NOTE: *One exhibitor makes bride and holiday*

NOTES

dolls. She sews and produces them as fast as she can. They are beautiful creation, and have been very successful. Her husband is her helper and they occupy a permanent booth at this Farmer's Market in Lake Worth, Florida.

4. Find out if the marketeers price-dicker with customers or allow their prices to be discounted.

5. Some markets start at 6:00 in the morning. You may have to be there earlier to obtain a choice location. Many of the choice spots go to regular vendors.

6. Be prepared for the sun, rain, snow, etc., if it is outside (Follow the suggestions under the previous chapter on craft shows etc.)

7. These shows are good TESTS for you, especially if other vendors have products like yours. Some flea markets handle second hand and junk items. Stay away from these.

3. MALL SHOWS

These are different from the average craft show. In malls throughout the country you will find "theme" shows at different times of the year. They could be jewelry, handicrafts, sewing, antique, home, toy, etc., shows. Many are well organized and draw exhibitors from far distances. I have talked to many of the participants; they follow the shows from state to state. They have been scheduled for months and even years ahead. Malls draw large crowds, the exposure is great, and so is the expense. The rent on your booth may be high. You may have to "man" the booth for long periods of time (10 to 10 each day). Start by inquiring at you local mall or plaza. A mall is better because it protects you from the elements.

There are few, if any, standards set by mall marketing directors in the past. The recession in the seventies brought a change of buying habits among mall shoppers. Mall merchants were feeling competition from the art/craft shows. As a result, many dropped them altogether. A major result of this period was the establishment of show standards. Tables were expected to be draped to the floor on all sides. No bed sheets were allowed and exhibitor dress codes were defined. Displays in general were improved. Exhibitors' signs were professionally done. The fees were thus increased drastically. This money went to the professional promoters who advertised and marketed the show. There are over 2000 malls in the country looking for ways to attract people . . . craft/art shows will bring them in.

NOTES

93

NOTES

94

4. CONSIGNMENTS

Here are some PROs and CONs of consigning products (putting your creation in a retail store without charging the owner UNLESS SOLD).

1. For the beginner it might be the ONLY way to get started.

2. Consign them ONLY to shoppes that you can physically visit.

3. Many stores change owners or go out of business. Be wary.

4. Your creation may very well be damaged or soiled.

5. Who pays for stolen merchandise?

6. Whose insurance covers fire, flood, etc. damage? Legally the product is still yours.

7. Will the store owner display and promote YOUR creation over their own or one with a greater profit margin?

8. You cannot give a better profit to consigned goods. You are the risk taker. We have seen 20 to 33% discount on consignment goods, any more is approaching desperation.

NOTES

9. Your record-keeping is increased.

10. You physically have to follow up for reorders or returns.

11. You are tying up a lot of capital (money) by LENDING your product to a store.

12. There are some successful area craft stores that can do wonders with your creation. Visit them and become friends.

13. A good rule of thumb — if the shop is over two years old you know they are successful (**MANY RETAIL BUSINESSES FAIL WITHIN 10 MONTHS**). There are the 10% that become winners. Start small with a few items, then leave more if they sell.

    Sara Addington from Birmingham, Georgia tells us that the only way she got started in her store was with consigned goods. She started with 15 or 20 products and now has over 200. Once she had proved herself, the craft people just poured in with their products.

14. There is some "shoddy merchandise" being made. You will have to sell the "quality" of your creation.

15. It helps to have a printed price list. (Type it and have it photocopied for pennies OR have it typeset and printed for still a nominal fee.) Example:

	one color	two color	three	four
Designer Pillow (small)	$12.00	15.00	17.50	22.50
Designer Pillow (medium)	$15.00	17.50	22.50	25.00
Designer Pillow (large)	$17.50	22.50	25.00	27.50
Designer Pillow (king)	$22.50	25.00	27.50	30.00

NOTES

Three or more .... less 10%
Six or more .... less 20%
Twelve or more .... less 33%
WE ACCEPT MASTER/VISA & PERSONAL CHECKS (U.S. funds)
PHONE ORDERS!!! 1-800-111-2222

SHIPPING CHARGE — add $2 to each pillow
ALL ORDERS SHIPPED WITHIN FIVE WORKING DAYS

100% SATISFACTION GUARANTEED If not completely satisfied send back (prepaid) undamaged goods for full refund.

NOTE: NOTICE U.S. funds only. If you get foreign money orders and checks paid in their country's funds you will be a loser IF their currency is less than ours. (Example: Canadian funds can cost you up to 25% less.)

PERSONAL CHECKS . . . We have found in the many years in business that we have been "stuck" with only 3 or 4 checks out of the hundreds we have processed. It seems that craft and mail order people are above average in honesty.

NOTE: Just read in Sunday's paper about a gal who specializes. She makes matching coats, boots and sunglasses for DOGS. She caters to the above-average pet owner, the Palm Beachers etc. Some have ordered up to twenty different costumes for their "mutts." She has even made tuxedos and formal gowns. Isn't this a great country! What opportunity for those who have imagination, persistance and desire.

I would strongly suggest a BLACK & WHITE photo of your product(s). A colored imprinted price list will cost more.

16. Have a consignment form and get everything in writing (NOT VERBAL). There are still some people who do business with a handshake; you may be able to someday also but until then CYA (Cover Your A--). GET IT IN WRITING. If you offer one shop a different deal than another, write it on the consignment form. (See Example)

CONSIGNMENT AGREEMENT

NAME OF RETAIL SHOP _____

ADDRESS _____ TELEPHONE _____

STATE _____ ZIP _____ OWNER _____

SUCCESS PUBLISHING/PERSON _____

ADDRESS _____ TELEPHONE _____

This agreement is between the shop and craftperson listed above.

DATE OF PLACEMENT _____ PERIOD OF TIME _____

RETAIL PRICE _____ WHOLESALE COST _____

1. The Retail price of the book will not be discounted.

2. Success Publishing agrees to pick up any UNDAMAGED products at the end of this agreement or at RENEWAL of the Consignment Time.

3. The store owner is responsible for any theft or damage to the consigned product.

4. Success Publishing will be paid for sold merchandise every thirty days, at the end of the agreement or whichever comes first.

ITEM	Retail Price	Store Profit	Due Success	Date Paid

NOTES

SIGNER RETAILER _____

SUCCESS _____ DATE _____

SUCCESS ADVERTISING & PUBLISHING CO.
Allan H. Smith, President
8084 Nashua Dr. Lake Park, FL 33410

No person or business remains the same; they either grow or shrink and die. For this reason you may have to consider selling in quantity to wholesalers, direct mailers, catalog houses, etc. Follow some of these rules and it may help you to approach quantity producing and selling more logically.

1. Establish a price list and stick to it.
2. Figure out your shipping costs and either include them in the price or charge extra.
3. Establish payment schedules and discounts.
4. Be able to talk the buyer's language.
5. Make it easy for the buyer to place an order.
6. Have order forms and purchase order numbers.
7. Understand purchase order numbers.
8. Offer 2% discount for payment within 30 days.
9. Show them the benefits — theirs, not yours — if they buy.
10. State your past sales successes.
11. Be prepared to state shipping dates and performance guarantees.

NOTES

12. If you grant exclusive rights or areas, state this.
13. If you have a minimum order, state this also.
14. Offer a sample and mark it as a sample or review copy.
15. Charge shipping except for large orders. Offer to prepay these charges.
16. State your return(s) policy.
17. Consider offering consignment for new accounts.
18. Have strict credit terms and stick by them.
19. Don't assume the customer will automatically order your goods. FOLLOW THROUGH with a call and ask for the order.
20. Have a catalog, price list, order forms and use them to sell again and again.

You may sell this way at a crafts show, a fair and other areas where the buyer comes to you. You may have to call on large accounts if you have a good sales success record. Use this to sell new accounts. Wholesalers are usually located in large cities. They expect you to make appointments with their buyers.

6. MANUFACTURERS

This is selling to the firms that make the products. What could you sell to them that will allow both of you to make money?

1. Patterns . . . are they patented?

2. Parts . . . which they would need for the finished product, parts that they could buy more cheaply than if they produced them themselves.

3. Ideas . . . make sure you have protected yours with a copyright.

4. Procedures . . . how to make something less expensively or faster than they are now doing.

It is unlikely that a manufacturer would buy a finished product from you BUT, if they do, then:

1. It would have to be cheaper than if they produced it.

2. The quantities would probably be humongous (super-large).

4. You would have to pay for shipping.

5. If successful, they would try to buy the next batch cheaper.

NOTES

7. RETAIL STORES

Here is a great way to distribute your items, although it will entail a lot more bookkeeping and door to door selling. You MUST formulate a price list BEFORE you sell to anyone. Here's an example:

FORMULATING A PRICE LIST

SUCCESS PUBLISHING
8084 Nashua Drive
Lake Park, Florida 33410
305/626-4643

WHOLESALE PRICE INFORMATION

1. The following are wholesale prices — for merchandise sold for resale only.

2. Tax exempt number must be included.

3. Minimum requirements are listed.

4. Prices are subject to change without notice.

5. Shipped: Freight FOB Lake Park, Florida.

6. No returns without prior permission.

7. Terms: NET 30 days after billing with approved credit.

8. No other discounts apply.

9. No COD orders.

10. Prices are for books distributed AND published by SUCCESS publishing ONLY.

11. For credit application.

COMPANY _____   ORDERED BY _____

ADDRESS _____ STATE _____ ZIP _____

TELEPHONE _____ BANK _____ ADDRESS _____

CREDIT REFERENCES: STATE _____

    1. NAME _____   PHONE _____

      ADDRESS _____

      STATE _____ ZIP _____

      CONTACT _____

    2. NAME _____   3. NAME _____

      ADDRESS _____   ADDRESS _____

      STATE _____ ZIP _____   STATE _____ ZIP _____

      CONTACT _____   CONTACT _____

TITLE	CATALOG #	RETAIL	WHOLESALE	TOTAL
TEENAGE MONEY MAKING GUIDE	301	$10.00		
HOW TO MAKE SCHOOL FUN	303	$14.95		
SEWING FOR PROFIT	305	$10.00		
HOW TO SELL YOUR CREATION	307	$11.95		
etc., etc.				

NOTES

One copy .... no discount
   2-11 .... 25% off retail
  12-24 .... 40% off retail
  25-49 .... 45% off retail
  50-99 .... 50% off retail
100 -399 .... 55% off retail
400-999 .... 50% + 25% off retail
1000 up .... contact us directly

8. CATALOG HOUSES

You probably receive many catalogs in the mail every year especially around Christmas time. These companies have to buy their supplies somewhere . . . IT COULD BE FROM YOU. How can you get your creation accepted?

1. Find out who the buyer is. You can do this by writing or calling and simply asking.

2. Find out the requirements to be interviewed. Will they do it via mail with a sample? Do you have to give it to a sales rep or does it have to be presented in person?

3. What are the discounts? Do they buy at 50%, 50 plus 25, or what? (Explanation . . . 50% plus 25% means that if you are selling an article for $10.00 then 50% off would mean $5.00. An additional 25% does not mean 25% of the $10.00 but of the remaining cost of $5.00 or 25% of $5 which is $1.25. Thus 50 plus 25 discount would mean $3.75 cost to the wholesaler or 62.5%.)

4. How many do they purchase initially? Are the quantities too large for you to produce practically? How about an order for 1000 hand-created Cabbage Patch doll sweaters and they want it in 30 days!

5. Will this increase in business affect your other accounts? It might be a "flash in the pan" and not last for any length of time.

6. It may be a BONANZA! It could change you from a small operator to a large entrepreneur.

7. Is your price protected and for how long when doing business with the company?

8. There are reference books in your library that lists many catalog houses. Write for information.

NOTES

9. CHAIN STORES

Another great potential outlet to sell your creation — Sears, K-Mart, Penney's, etc. Consider chain convenience stores, chain drug stores, gas-food marts, any place that sells retail. Some tips:

1. Find out the place of buying and the buyer who buys your kind of thing.

2. Make an appointment. DON'T go in unannounced.

3. Go in well prepared, with the prices that you want to sell for. DON'T let them talk you down on the retail. You do know how much it is worth. Know how much discount you will give. Be realistic, do a little research and find out what they are currently paying.

4. Follow some of the suggestions under selling to catalog houses.

5. If you knock on enough doors, a lot will open and ask you in to buy your product. Just how much do you want to be successful?

6. Make sure your product is protected from copy-cats as well as possible with copyrights or patents.

7. Establish a return policy. Many like to have a 10% return charge or do it free. Your reputation will follow you . . . BE FAIR.

8. Be prepared to give datings. These are longer periods of time to pay their bill IF credit-established. Some merchants will buy Christmas merchandise in April, have it shipped in July and pay for it next January.

9. Be prepared to give samples to the buyers. This will remind them of your product and give them time to inspect it.

NOTES

10. Remember it sometimes takes 2-3 visits to SELL a buyer. Don't get discouraged.

11. Have promotional materials that will help them sell your product.

    a. Poster

    b. Window Signs

    c. Pre-prepared Ads

    d. Displays etc.

    3. Names of customers who have bought the product.

102

10. DIRECT MAIL

Many of these principles are listed under the chapter on advertising. Selling by direct mail means transmitting the description of your product to the public via the mail. This could be by:

1. Catalogs — yours or someone else's.

2. One or two page slinger/brochure.

3. Magazine with your ad in it.

4. Newspaper, newsletter with your message included.

5. Pennysaver or shopping guide.

6. A letter or a post card with your sales message in it.

7. An insert in a newspaper, magazine or newsletter.

Follow "How to create an Ad" in the advertising chapter. Where do you get the addresses to mail your catalog, slinger, brochure, letter or announcement? What to then do?

1. Form your own mailing list created by "teaser" ads or from collecting addresses.

2. Network or exchange with another craft/home worker.

3. Rent from a list house. I would not recommend this. I have rented from them. Some are good; some "seed" the lists with garbage.

4. You have to remember that 20-25% of all people move in a year. That means that 25% of a list is no good after a year. If you spend money on brochures, postage, etc., this could waste a lot of money if you do not have a FRESH UPDATED CLEAN list.

5. If you do rent a list, rent the minimum. Test it with first class postage. You will get back the expired addresses. With bulk-mailings (3rd class) you do not get back the undeliverable mail, thus you never know if the advertisement reached the person or is thrown away undelivered by the post office. Take a look at the undelivered mail in the post office dumpsters.

6. Some say that 20% of bulk mailings are lost, damaged or destroyed by the post office. If you add on 20%-25% attrition, it totals 40% . . . meaning four out of ten that you mail never get there. This just about doubles your direct mailing cost.

7. If you "rent" a list it is for one time only. You are not allowed to use the names and addresses again without paying another rental fee. How do they know? They "seed" the list with addresses so they can check for people who use them again without paying.

8. A natural for your home computer. Store it and print your own mailing labels on your word processor.

9. At a craft show, raffle away something you'll have all the names, addresses — good prospects.

LETS TAKE A LOOK AT THE COST TO SEND 5,000 Slingers Advertising your products. First a couple of important facts:

1. You should average $20/order to make it pay.

2. A 1½% return (75 orders from 5000 mailed) is considered about average Under this is poor. Over 2% or 100 orders are GREAT!

3. Be sure to charge state tax if your state charges it and if the customer is from your state.

4. The best months to mail out advertisements via direct mail are late January, early February and July.

5. Start to plan 4-6 months BEFORE you want to mail out your material.

6. Consider mailing by bulk mail (around 13¢ as of 1985) or by first class (22¢).

7. If you mail out bulk yourself, you have to get a yearly bulkmailing permit (about $45).

8. If you do bulk mailings you will have to sort the mail by zip-code and deliver to the post office packaged in zip code order.

9. Remember once you send out a bulk mailing you never know if it got there. With first class you get the non-deliverable back

WHAT WILL IT COST?

5000 addresses rented @ 60/M	$300
5000 slingers printed	200
5000 envelopes	150
5000 order cards	75
5000 return envelopes	125
5000 22¢ stamps	(1100)
5000 13¢ bulk mailings	(650)
	$1950 Or $1500

NOTES

A 1½% return at an average of $20/ responses will generate

1.5 x 5000 = 75 responses
75 x $20 = $1500
To make any money you must do 2% or better
2 x 5000 = 100 responses
100 x $20 = $2000

IMPORTANT!!!!! KEEP ALL OF YOUR CUSTOMERS NAMES AND ADDRESSES. These become your mailing list for mailings.

10. Choose a good product of acceptable quality and have something that people need.

11. Try to select a product in considerable demand—or an unusual or unique product difficult to get elsewhere, that individual retailers can't afford to carry because of the small local demand (adding up, however, to large national demand).

12. Try to tie up the source of your product to reduce competition; perhaps a product generally in short supply but available to you; brand-new merchandise has an edge over standard catalog items.

13. Develop a line; you will probably never get rich on one item. Use a succession of items.

14. Use colorful, imaginative, practical, hard-wearing, proper-size packaging.

15. Check competing transportation (mail, freight, etc.), and use cheapest.

16. Watch shipping weight so that slight excess doesn't boost shipping cost into next higher bracket.

17. Guarantee postage so that the post office will notify the addressee.

18. A reliable supplier is really the keystone of a mail order operation that will guarantee his output for quality and volume. He will make small deliveries at first, and step up production as needed.

19. Price should be fair. Figure in prepaid postage.

20. Use round numbers — preferably one coin or one bill (not odd-cent prices) for convenience in remitting.

21. Offer money back; so figure in this cost, too.

22. Determine your break-even point accurately

23. Figure in *all* costs: unit cost of product, itself; cost of depositing checks, wrapping, transportation, postage, damage, rejects, replacements, c.o.d. costs, refusals, bad debts, normal business overhead.

24. Get correct ratio of selling price to cost of product (generally 4 to 1).

25. Don't limit yourself to low-priced merchandise; markup is too small to be profitable.

26. Be ready to advertise continuously, or don't even start in business.

27. Start with small space.

28. If you have something real good, use large space.

29. Suit your advertising to the medium carrying it to appeal to its audience.

30. Base your budget and schedule on ad pull by months.

31. Don't be afraid to experiment; vary ad size or time, copy and appeal, check and double-check to find right advertising slang and selling appeals.

32. Try split-run testing if available.

33. Use special gimmicks, such as gift appeals, holidays, quantity discounts, etc.

34. Base your advertising budget on the number of inquiries needed to make the ads pay.

35. Pulling power of one ad over another may vary as much as 25 to 1.

36. Conventional selling cost by mail is 15% compared with 3 to 4% for retailers' ad budgets, but repeat orders make mail order profitable.

NOTES

105

37. Milk a successful ad by repeating it until diminishing returns set in.

38. Get editorial mentions in shopping sections of media.

39. Use a practical, how-to approach, tight copy.

40. White space is less important for mail order than for prestige advertising.

41. Write copy for a mass audience — write as you speak, use simple, selling copy—not stylized.

42. Avoid tricky phrases; be sincere; don't exaggerate, use the you approach.

43. Convince the reader that you are dependable and reliable, make it easy for the prospect to act — give simple, specific directions.

44. Don't try institutional or goodwill copy, just sell.

45. Analyze readership studies to develop copy techniques.

46. Use short testimonials to plug products and company.

47. Play up local or regional fame, like well-known fruit areas, Williamsburg craft shops, Southern delicacies.

48. Guarantee product and satisfaction; always offer return privilege.

49. Perhaps offer something free as a premium or bonus.

50. Key all ads to test pull.

51. Check and double-check copy for possible omissions, unclear facts, ambiguous information, confusing directions.

52. Use appropriate illustration — selling pictures, not for art's sake.

NOTES

53. Be sure to include photo or clear drawing with detailed copy, particularly if product is complicated.

54. Bold headlines and other devices outpull cheesecake.

55. Consult other mail order users, agencies, and media on best media for you.

56. Make sure you are in a media company that is good for your product.

57. For quick pilot test, quick return, early check on copy pull, use radio or newspapers; for the long pull, use magazines, list from your inquiries and customers, reputable list houses or mail order advertisers.

58. Rent your lists to noncompeting mail order companies and direct-mail houses.

59. Keep your mailing lists restricted as much as possible to read prospects.

60. Ask for cash or checks, preferably not c.o.d.; but don't advertise no c.o.d.'s, accept checks—few bounce.

61. Obtain necessary papers to legalize checks made out to every possible variation of your company name.

62. Avoid the phrase, *BILL ME*, in coupon or order form.

63. Remember: The customer is always right,

64. Take care of complaints quickly, make replacement or adjustment immediately.

65. Don't be afraid to write a courteous, explanatory letter.

66. Make immediate refunds at no cost to the customer, adjust overpayments quickly.

67. Repeat business is vital to success; keep the customer sold, it take a long time to build audience confidence in buying by mail.

68. Be prompt and courteous in answering inquiries, shipping order, explaining delays, making adjustments, refunding money.

69. Personalize all correspondence with signed letters.

70. Follow up initial sale with mailing pieces, folders, catalogs, brochures, etc.

71. At intervals mail new price lists to customers to encourage new business.

72. Ask satisfied customers to submit names of friends, neighbors, relatives, or business associates as potential customers, and offer a bonus for this.

73. Run a good piece of merchandise and work good mailing lists as long as they pay; then try them again later.

74. Be ready to answer all sorts of byproduct mail, offers, inquiries, deals and so forth.

75. Based on a keying system keep accurate records of the pull of each ad showing effectiveness of various combinations of headline, art, copy, medium, and so forth.

76. Offer catalogs if line is big enough, but charge small sum or restrict distribution to active customers to increase catalog value to them and save you money.

77. Don't be surprised if there are ups and downs depending on the seasons, days of the month, or competition from tax payments, and so forth.

78. Don't expect many returns after the first six months, but don't be surprised if orders or inquiries trickle in for years.

NOTES

107

11. CO-OP MAILINGS

Find out all you can about newsletters and other crafters in the same catagory as yours. Network with them. Ask if you can send out a slinger/brochure with their newsletter or catalog. Offer, of course, to pay for this service OR do the same for them. I just recently found a person who had a newsletter with the same interests as one of my books. She mailed out 15,000 of my catalogs stapled to her N/L. for a very reasonable fee. The returns were fabulous. She then offered to send out 5,000 more catalogs at no extra charge. As I am writing this I said to myself, "Here's a great example of someone doing a little bit extra for you. Why not do something for her?" I picked up the phone and called Gail Kibinger, editor of SEW GREAT NEWSLETTER (as of 1985,$1/year) Box 6146, South Bend, Indiana 46660. I offered to include an advertisement in my next catalog free of charge and felt good that we both could help each other.

NOTES

You will find many publications and businesses that will be glad to share with you.

There are some that have never thought of various kinds of promotions. Get in touch with them and make a deal . . . all they can do is say no.

You can pay to have your slinger/brochure included in pennysavers, shoppers guides and of course your daily newspapers. If you decide to insert it in your daily paper, remember you are competing with Sears, K-Mart and scores of other biggies. This does not mean that the consumer will not read your material, just that they have a lot to look at BEFORE seeing yours. The last time I checked the cost it was around 1-2¢ per paper. You can also designate the area you want included.

12. HOLIDAY/HOME SHOWS

In the book SEWING FOR PROFITS I mentioned the two gals who hold Christmas Craft show every year in one of their homes. They have been doing it for years now and do about $10,000 worth of business in a 3-4 week time.

There are many kinds of Home Shows. You are familiar with Tupperware, Amway etc. There are even toy, sex-apparel, book, clothes, homedecorating items, hardware — you name it, someone has tried it. The important thing to remember is how well it is done, the quality of merchandise and the price. The two girls who have the Christmas show combine the talents of many other crafts peopls. They sell display space and take a percentage of the sales. There is a waiting list to be included. You can start the same thing. Let's lay down some basic groundwork and suggestions:

NOTES

1. Determine IF you can handle the interruption of your normal (or abnormal) family routine.

2. Get the cooperation of the other family members,

3. Decide WHERE you will display the products. In the cellar, garage, attic, barn, family room, porch, etc. Once you decide, plan to clear the area(s) of all other things that could be stolen, damaged or in the way.

4. You may start with only yourself and a few other craftspeople.

5. Find a way to let others know what you are offering. In other words, you can have a great set-up, beautiful displays, the right prices, but no one knows about it. Your P.R. promotional work is just as important as what you are selling. Read the chapter on Free and Low Cost promotions for ideas.

6. Start in early enough to make enough products to display and/or sell. Some "creators" sell from samples, they make specific sold orders.

7. Don't make too much noise or "shake the bush" too hard. The neighbors might become envious or jealous and turn you in, (if there is someone to turn you in to). A good way, I have found, is to include the immediate neighbors if you can. If the traffic is heavy, you may have people parking on their property.

8. I am pretty sure that you do not have to have a special permit to sell or have a selling-party in your home.

9. Offer something to get the consumer there:

   a. A door prize. (good way . . . have them register their names and addresses . . . you can use these for your mailing lists).

   b. Light refreshments.

   c. A craft celebrity.

d. Free Samples

e. Instructional Catalogs/slingers/brochures

f. Instructional course/seminar/class . . . ever notice the craft/hobby/art stores? They always have classes, a lot of times FREE if you buy products there.

g. Special discounts.

h. Free gift wrapping.

i. Items that are not available anywhere else.

10. Clearly mark every item with pilfer-proof labels. A good way is to include the cost and date on the label (See the chapter on labeling and packaging)

11. If others are displaying and are not part of your Co-op, charge them for their spare. Don't overdo it. Maybe $25 per day. Also take a percentage of the sales. 10% would be fair. If you do this, handle all of the money yourself.

12. Inspect and research other co-op craft selling operations. You can get a lot of ideas.

13. Start 4-5 months ahead of time. Carefully plan, budget and organize. (See chapter on planning).

14. Have a theme or reason . . . just like a cocktail party. It could be:

a. Christmas
b. Valentine's Day
c. Easter
d. Spring, Summer, Winter, Fall
e. Going back to school
f. Getting ready for vacation

g. Mother's, Father's Day
h. Christmas in July
i. Halloween/Thanksgiving
j. Super Bowl/World Series
k. Wedding/Birthday/Anniversary gift
l. Leisure time

NOTES

15. Establish a price schedule and don't allow people to dicker price with you. (unless you want to).

16. Identify your product with enough labels, brochures, catalogs etc. Make sure you get every person's address.

17. Display the space items attractively. Make the whole area comfortable.

18. I would recommend the elimination of places to sit, people will waste space and time. You could have an area to write up the orders. Such as a desk or order table.

19. Eliminate smoking, watch what you serve for refreshments. People do have accidents and may soil or damage the sale goods.

20. You may want to serve refreshments in the kitchen only.

21. Try to control the traffic. I have seen it directed in one door, past the merchandise and out another door with a cashier at the end. The more you can minimize confusion and disorder, the more you will sell and the better feelings your guests will have.

22. Record all of your sales and give a receipt. This is a good time to hand out P.R. material about the products. Sometimes people read them later, come back or send in an order. A catalog or a list of items you have will move it easy for repeat sales.

23. If possible, mention on a poster and on a slinger, date of the next show.

24. This is a good chance to have a "comment card" for the participants to fill in. It will give you a wealth of information:

```
┌────────────────────────────────────────────────────────────────────┐
│                                                                      │
│  NAME & ADDRESS _____         │
│                                                                      │
│                 _____         │
│                                                                      │
│  WHERE DID YOU HEAR ABOUT OUR PRESENTATION? _____         │
│  WHAT DID YOU HEAR ABOUT OUR PRESENTATION? _____         │
│  WHAT DID YOU LIKE MOST ABOUT OUR SHOW? _____         │
│  WHAT COULD WE DO TO IMPROVE IT? _____         │
│  WHAT OTHER KINDS OF MERCHANDISE WOULD YOU HAVE LIKED TO HAVE         │
│  SEEN? _____         │
│  I WOULD BE INTERESTED IN BEING CALLED PERSONALLY WHEN THE NEXT       │
│  SHOW IS PLANNED . . . PHONE _____ .       │
│                                                                      │
└────────────────────────────────────────────────────────────────────┘
```

25. Try to get a head count of how many came. You can then determine what percent bought something.

26. Figure out how many bought items and for how much. Then average the sales. Example: if 100 people bought merchandise totalling $1000, then each person spent $10 as an average.

27. You may be able to pass out other craft/hobby creators' sales messages and charge a fee.

28. I have seen some people paid for passing out manufacturers' sales literature (sewing machine products, national magazines, etc.).

29. Call the local papers and ask the social editor if the event would be worth mentioning in their paper. They are constantly looking for human interest stores. Of course a lot of exposure would encourage competition.

30. As soon as it is over, sit down and record all of the comments, ideas, mistakes and successes you had. Great ideas for the next show.

NOTES

111

13. BROCHURE

All through this book I have mentioned a brochure, a slinger or a catalog. You must have something to constantly remind the customer about your product(s). You cannot show your creation to every potential purchaser. The next best thing is a description of it. The description has to "sell" the customer. It has to make them want to buy. You and I get hundreds of "descriptions" of products every week in the mail. We see them on television, in magazines, newspapers, billboards and even have people knocking on our doors and ringing our phones to tell us about their products. You have to do this also. The quality of your sales material must be good enough to get the public to look at and to read and hopefully take action . . . To buy! Follow me through some steps that may help you to produce a good message.

1. Decide on what kind of promotional piece you want to use — a brochure (3 or more pages), a slinger (just one or two sides of a page), a catalog (multiple pages of multiple items).

2. Determine how you are going to use it — hand it out, leave it on a display case, mail it, include in with other papers etc.

3. Get an estimate of how much it will cost to produce 100, 1,000, 5,000, 100,000. As you already know, it costs less per piece the more you have printed or photocopied.

NOTES

4. Consider having it typed or type-set and have it photocopied (check both prices).

5. You may find that having it printed on a pastel or odd color will attract the consumer's eye faster than using plain white.

6. Check the prices of paper. Your reputation goes with your sales message. For a little more you could use a quality bond or a semi-gloss, paper.

7. You can save money and get a two-colors effect by having your paste-up or graphic artist make part of it screened. This makes a half color, great for two or three color brochures.

8. If you are selling your brochure, you can use your tax-exempt number and not pay tax, for printing. You then must charge appropriate tax on all sales in your county or state.

9. You should use an illustration or photo. People will be attracted much more to your message. Use black and white photos and illustrations. It will save a lot on printing.

10. Consider making your brochure a self-contained "mailing price." I have done this many times with brochures for some of the seminars I conduct. I fold the 8½ x 11 or 8¼ x 14 paper into three equal parts. One third of one side of a page I use for the mailing labels.

    This saves the stuffing and expense of an envelope. (See Example).

11. Draw up a few ideas and test them on your family or friends. What do they like? I do this with the colors of my book covers. The family usually picks the one they like. I do this every time I have to choose a tie before dressing. Of course I have a shirt on!

12. Reflect yourself, your product, your enthusiasm in your message.

13. ALWAYS! ALWAYS! give the benefits the consumer will recieve IF they buy your product. Make them want it! Show them how their lives will be better IF they buy it! PEOPLE DON'T BUY PRODUCTS. THEY BUY SOLUTIONS TO PROBLEMS!

NOTES

Turn Your Talent Into Money

G

■ HOW TO SELL YOUR HOMEMADE CREATION — Allan Smith

Just published, this is a book for those with talent, for those who have created something they want to show or sell to the world. A guide for those who have to start small and with limited money. Written with twenty years experience in successful home-based and self-marketing businesses. It will walk you through the basics of selling your product to the consumer. Where and how to find free or low cost publicity, how to create an appealing ad, how to name, price, package and mail your product. It lists 25 different market areas and over 100 places that might buy your creation. This 200 page 8½ x 11 manual will save you hours of wasted effort and many dollars in wasted cash. This is the first step when considering going in business for yourself.

Success Publications • 200 pages
L.C. 84-51623
ISBN 0-931113-01-6
Soft Cover $10.00
8½ x 11

H

■ 901 SUPER QUICK SEWING TIPS — Artefabes

A TREASURE CHEST of SEWING SECRETS and all those "GOOD LITTLE THINGS" that help you "ZIP" it up for wearing tomorrow! • HOW TO sew FASTER and BETTER. • In the NEW REVISED Super Quick Sewing Tips, we've added 600 NEW TIPS, fun ideas and suggestions to the original 350. • Before winding thread onto the bobbin, run first 8" across a different color crayon, four or five times. Crayon color will alert you when the bobbin thread is about to run out. • Easy hand hemming . . . Place pins on right side of the garment after hem has been pressed into place. Threads won't catch on the pins. Saves time. • Avoid tragedy by placing a pin at each end of a buttonhole before slashing. • If working on dark fabric and it's hard to remove stitching, run chalk lightly over stitches. They will show up for easy removal. • Whether you're "new" or "experienced" 901 SUPER QUICK SEWING TIPS is FOR YOU! Organized and cross-indexed so you can turn to any subject in seconds. Over 900 illustrations.

Sew Kno-How
$9.95

I

■ SEWING, THE COMPLETE GUIDE — HP Books

GET READY! GET SET! GET SEWING! A practical guide for everyday comprehensive reference. Sewing techniques from A to Z . . . learn about collars, cuffs, bases, pockets, zippers, hems, sleeves and much much more. Learn how to choose patterns, make body measurements, prepare fabric. Discusses layout, cutting, marking stitches and threads. How to purchase clothes and recycle old garments. Over 1000 step by step illustrations, basic and advanced secrets. YOU'LL WONDER HOW YOU EVER GOT ALONG WITHOUT IT!

HP Books • 176 pages
ISBN 0-89586-253-0
$7.95

SATISFACTION GUARANTEED
Your Money Back
If Not Completely
Satisfied (Returned
In Saleable Condition)
Postpaid

Limited Time!
FREE
Doll/Sewing Source & Supply Catalog
For First 300 Orders
$6.95 Value

**All Orders
Shipped
Postpaid
No
Extra Charges**

Success Publishing
8084 Nashua Drive
Lake Park, FL 33410
(305) 626-4643

ORDER FORM
Please send me the following I've checked below:

Name _____ Phone( ) _____

Address _____ State_____ Zip_____

Mail to: Success Publishing (305) 626-4643
8084 Nashua Dr., Lake Park, FL 33410

QUANTITY	CODE	TITLE	PRICE	TOTAL
	A	Teenage Moneymaking Guide	$10.00	
	B	Catalog Sources for Creative People	7.95	
	C	Sew & Save Source Book	9.95	
	D	Homemade Money	12.95	
	E	How to Make School Fun	10.00	
	F	Sewing For Profits	10.00	
	G	How to Sell Your Homemade Creation	10.00	
	H	901 Super Quick Sewing Tips	9.95	
	I	Sewing, The Complete Guide	7.95	

☐ Payment Enclosed (U.S. funds)

☐ Charge Master/Visa _____ Signature

Card Number _____ Exp. Date

114

CLIP AND SEND NOW!

SHIPPED! POSTPAID

MONEY BACK GUARANTEE!

Treat Yourself and Your Friends To These Top-Flight Books

A

■ TEENAGE MONEYMAKING GUIDE — Allan Smith

A book for those who would like to make money on their own. Years of research provides information for 101 money making opportunities. It gives the reader motivation to be a winner in life by being their own boss. The young entrepreneur is shown the possible costs, time, materials and recommendations before, during and after the job is over. The 281 pages are jam-packed with 136 illustrations, 50 actual success stories and 12 basic secrets of business. It has been proven that employed people are benefits to themselves and the community they live in. The F.B.I. states that 33% of major crimes committed in the U.S. are by unemployed teenagers. This guide can help shape productive futures.

WINNER'S MAKE IT HAPPEN, LOSER'S STAND AROUND AND ASK, "WHAT HAPPENED."

Success Publications •
281 pages
L.C. 84-90126
ISBN 0-931113-00-8
Soft Cover $10.00
5½ x 8½

★ 101 Ways to Start Your Own Business
★ Be Your Own Boss
★ 12 Secrets to Success

B

■ CATALOG SOURCES FOR CREATIVE PEOPLE — Margaret Boyd

CATALOG SOURCES FOR CREATIVE PEOPLE offers more than 2000 places to find patterns, plans, kits and materials for all sorts of hobbies, arts and crafts! This is the fifth and most comprehensive craft supply directory compiled by Margaret A. Boyd, a talented artisan and writer of how-to crafts articles. Margaret's frustration — the availability of craft and hobby supplies led her to collect and organize catalogs and brochures from companies across the United States. Now she is sharing this wealth of information with crafts people everywhere! Each detailed listing is categorized by specific craft or hobby for easy reference. Information includes company name and address, catalog or brochure if available, products or services offered, special discounts and mail order plans.

HP Books • 224 pages
ISBN 0-89586-130-5
Soft Cover $7.95
8½ x 11

C

■ THE SEW AND SAVE SOURCE BOOK — Margaret Boyd

The most complete and comprehensive directory ever of mail order supplies for creative and utility sewing by hand or machine. You'll find products and materials you never knew existed . . . products that will trigger your imagination and add new creative outlets for your present skills. Not just a catalog, this guide also provides scores of tips to add the most professional look to your art — whether you are finishing a buttonhole, assembling a doll, or insulating a window shade. Here are just some of the areas covered: • Basic supplies (many at discount) • Tools, aids, and equipment for hand and machine sewing • Fabrics and leathers • Trims and fillers • "Wet Decorating" supplies: paint, stencil, screen, dye, stamp • Specialty sewing supplies: embroidery, smocking, quilting • Infants' and children's wear and accessories • Adult fashions • Historic and ethnic clothing • Holiday wear • Sports and outdoor wear and accessories • Bridal and wedding styles and accessories • Decorative home accessories • Personal accessories • Soft sculpture • Dolls and toy making • Miniatures • Bath and bedroom linens • Holiday and "special occasion" home decorative accessories • Furniture and upholstery • Outdoor and camping gear • Supportive materials, products, and services • Educational media: films, tapes, home study courses • Booksellers • Consumer and trade publications • Organizations, associations, and other resource groups.

Betterway Publications •
216 pages
ISBN 0-932620-23
Soft Cover $9.95
8½ x 11

D

■ HOMEMADE MONEY — Barbara Brabec

This book clearly shows you how to get started in business and to pick the one that's right for you. Plan for success and build a pathway to profit. How to price products and services, sell direct to consumers, wholesalers and consignments. How to get the most out of limited advertising. How to diversify your business and multiply profits. It has three books in one. A comprehensive "Marketing Bible" with trade-secrets from professionals. An encyclopedic A to Z "Crash Course" in Business Basics, everything you need to feel secure. A mind boggling 500 listing RESOURCE DIRECTORY that brings together for the first time, important resources for the homebased workers in all fields.

Betterway Publications
• 272 pages
ISBN 0-932620-31-0
$12.95 • 8½ x 11

E

■ HOW TO MAKE SCHOOL FUN — Allan H. Smith

This book is for the parent or child that needs help accepting school. 76% of surveyed school children stated that they did not like going to school. Whose fault is it? It could be the school system and it could be the attitude of the parent and/or student. Loaded with chapters on building self confidence, getting acceptance by peers, getting teachers on your side, how to be popular and well-liked. How to turn around those DULL classes, boring teachers, restless bus rides, un-imaginable P.E. classes and tasteless lunches. How to get involved, coordinate work, home and school. How to earn and save money, should I drop out? and much, much more. FINALLY! a book that tells it like it is and how to improve and capitalize on those productive young years of school life.

Success Publications •
200 pages
L.C. 84-90227
ISBN 0-931113-03-2
Soft Cover $10.00
5½ x 8½

F

■ SEWING FOR PROFITS — Judy and Allan Smith

SEWING FOR PROFITS created especially for those with the desire to market and sell their creation. Questions such as: Is going into business for me?, Do I have the necessary talent, enthusiasm, resources and preparation?, How do I correctly buy materials and market my creation?, are answered. This is a must for those contemplating the start of a business in sewing and craft items. The authors have spent over twenty years in the retail, teaching, publishing and production of sewing and craft creations. The public is anxious to buy new and exciting products. Selling to the consumer can be a costly and frustrating experience. With proper direction, such as outlined in SEWING FOR PROFITS, many talented and creative people can be guided to success. In this book, the reader is gently escorted through the necessary steps to operate a successful business.

PEOPLE DON'T BUY PRODUCTS, THEY BUY SOLUTIONS TO PROBLEMS.

Success Publications
111 pages
L.C. 84-51623
ISBN 0-931113-01-6
Soft Cover $10.00
5½ x 8

• Turn Your Creative Talent into Money
• A Practical Yet Sensitive and Creative
• Learn How Professionals Do It

115

EXAMPLE OF BROCHURE

Many Employers use the excuse that teenagers are too young, too inexperienced, too immature and many other negative reasons.

As a result many skilled and ambitious young people remain unemployed.

The Federal Bureau of Labor states the following unemployment figures for the 16-19 age group:

White 21%
Black 48%
Hispanic 30%

The F.B.I. 1982 Report shows that over 33% of major crimes in the U.S. involves unemployed teenagers.

Allan Smith has written a guide for young teenagers that presents opportunities for these people to start and operate their own business. To expose them to the feeling of accomplishment, self satisfaction & success.

NOTES

THE WORLD IS MADE UP OF WINNERS AND LOSERS. BEING IN THEIR OWN BUSINESS, EARNING THEIR OWN MONEY AND BEING THEIR OWN BOSS CAN MAKE A PERSON A WINNER. IT TAKES DETERMINATION AND PERSISITANCE TO BE SUCCESSFUL. WINNERS *"MAKE IT HAPPEN,"* LOSERS STAND AROUND AND ASK. *"WHAT HAPPENED."*

(EXAMPLE OF BROCHURE)

The Teenage Moneymaking Guide will give the tools to make it happen. It shows how others have made fortunes working for themselves!

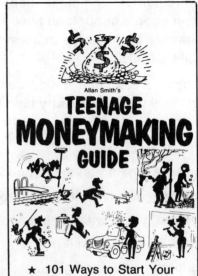

THEY WILL LEARN:

• **HOW MUCH IT WILL COST TO GET STARTED**
• **HOW TO GET START UP MONEY**
• **WHAT TO DO BEFORE THEY START**
• **"HELPFUL HINTS" TO MAKE THE JOB EASIER**
• **HOW TO GET REFERRALS AND RECOMMENDATIONS**

• **THE EASY WAY TO GET CUSTOMERS**
    AND MUCH, MUCH MORE . . .

PLEASE SEND: **NOTES**

☐ Review copy ($10 less 50%) $5.00
☐ Additional copies ($10 less 25%) $7.50

_____

☐ Enclosed payment
☐ Bill us   Total _____

Name _____

Title _____

School _____

School Systems _____

Address _____   **117**

State _____ Zip _____

SEND TO:

SUCCESS PUBLISING
8084 Nashua Drive
Lake Park, FL 33410

14. DOOR TO DOOR

Here is the great American way of selling and probably the hardest and most unappealing. Many of the greatest people in our land have started this way. You will have to be prepared to accept rejections and rude people.

It has been stated that if you can be successful selling this way you can sell anything to anyone.

1. Make sure you are prepared to sell or present whatever you have.

2. Make sure the item(s) are in good condition.

3. Make sure you have a printed price list or estimate.

4. Dress neatly and with confidence.

5. Always use the sidewalk(s)

6. Ring three times, then give up.

7. If there is no answer, leave a brochure, calling card and write a note stating you were there.

8. Beware of dogs.

9. Have a smile on your face when the door is open.

10. Greet with smiles and a greeting . . . "Good Morning" etc.

NOTES

118

11. If possible, greet them with their names. You can see it on the mailbox or ask the neighbor the name of the people next door. What an impression this makes! "The sweetest sound in any language is the sound of your own name."

12. Hold the item, brochure, price list up high so the person instantly recognizes what you are selling.

13. ALWAYS have a reference from one of their neighbors or friends to give you credibility.

14. Realize that you will get refusals. Learn to accept them as a rejection of the goods you are selling, not of you personally.

15. Always treat everyone with courtesy. You will meet some mean people; just thank them for their time and leave.

16. Explain the BENEFIT(S) to the customer . . . "This will do this for you!"

17. Ask for an order after explaining.

18. Many times it is a good idea to get a deposit; be sure to issue a receipt.

19. Follow through with the delivery or work on time.

20. Keep a card system, stating what was done during the presentation.

21. Ask for referrals even when the person refuses. Ask if they know of anyone who can use your product or service.

22. Be proud of your item or service and show the customer you are.

23. Pick the neighborhood that looks as if it would use or buy your product.

24. Think about traveling in pairs, for safety and for self-assurance.

25. If you can't sell them, leave them with a good feeling AND your brochure or catalog.

15. PREMIUM/GIVE-AWAY

Many banks, supermarkets, organizations give potential customers something free. They want them as customers or want to sell them some other product, membership or service. I have heard about authors who have sold 100,000's of books to banks, to theme parks, to super department stores to give away. Think about it.

* Homemade hand-forged knife . . . free with membership to Boy Scouts.

* Hand-etched ceramic beer mug with name and emblem . . . to every new American Legion member.

* Hand-made apron with name . . . to every participant in Cooking Class or Seminar.

* FREE Hand-sewn typewriter cover with the purchase of "XYZ TYPING BOOK,"

* FREE cover for computer and word processor . . . with purchase of computer.

* FREE crocheted hot-pan holders with every set of SEARS TEFLON PANS.

* Your Name in calligraphy on door on dashboard with the purchase of any 1986 CHEVROLET from BROWN'S GMC CAR LOT.

* FREE dog sweater (hand-made) with the purchase of any of our dogs.

* Hand-carved name plate for every new employee.

There are any number of possibilities for your product. . . USE YOUR INGENUITY AND IMAGINATION.

"To make a lot of money, find a new product" . . . Aristotle Onassis.

16. ORGANIZATIONAL . . . RAFFLES, DOOR PRIZES

The Elks, Lions, Kiwanis, Rotary, Optimists all look for gimmicks to get members to the meetings OR to find new ones. They also need money to continue to exist. MAKE THEM AN OFFER THEY CANNOT REFUSE. Offer to make them so many products for so much money. They can raffle them, give them away as a bonus or offer then as door prizes. They have to be appealing and useable by the members of their families. You wouldn't want to give pink head scarves to the Steel Workers Union 298 or hand-created belt buckle to the Ladies Lace-Embroidery Club.

* Coffee or beer mug with the club's emblem AND the member's name (In the Roycroft Inn in East Aurora, N.Y., they used to have glass mugs hanging over the bar. Each one was etched with a customer's name. They had paid a fee to belong to this certain club. One of the "perks" was this "drinking glass." It made the customer feel important AND brought them back time and time again.)

* Name tags, handmade out of wood, plastic, whatever.

* A woven rug, embroidered wall flag with the club's emblem.

* Neckties or scarves with the organization's emblem.

NOTES

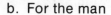

17. GIFT OF THE MONTH

A lot of money is being made on club of the months . . . books, records, meats, fruits, flowers etc. Why not create twelve different gifts, (or get together with others) and form a Unique Gift of the Month service? . . . Some ideas:

    a. Business people . . . hand-carved name plaque, hand-drawn/painted calendar, original Christmas cards, ceramic name coffee mug, hand-made computer or typewriter dust covers

    Leather-covered appointment book, etc.

    b. For the man   e. For the professional (medical)

    c. For the woman   f. For the professional (accountant, attorney, stock broker)

    d. For the teacher

Gather as many fellow craft/business people as necessary to each contribute gifts. You be the king-pin. Give them so much for each creation.

Now you have to market this unique GIFT OF THE MONTH service. You will have to have a distinctive ad and place it in spots when specific people will see it:

NOTES

    a. The business section of the newspaper

    b. The hospital newsletter

    c. The company bulletin

    d. The club monthly paper.

    e. The local law journal

    f. A penny saver or shopping guide etc.

Pick the media that will get to the type of person right for the type of gift you are offering.

You may have to gather twelve samples and sell door-to-door, business-to-business or office-to-office. You could set up a display table at a craft show.

18. PARTY PLAN

You must have been to a Tupperware house party or one like it within the last couple of years. Why not a craft party plan? You could gather from other sources and display them at your house. Follow some of the suggestions under "Holiday/Home Shows." You should have unique, one-of-a-kind type products to offer to those attending. Test first to see how well accepted they are. Have you received positive feedback? Have you had a good experience displaying at a craft show? You have had a good experience displaying at a craft show? You have to find a source of your attendees. You may do it through referrals OR send invitations to a certain group of people. You may get membership rolls from a garden club, a church group, etc. Ask permission and invite them. A good way to make it beneficial to them is to offer a rebate of say 10% to their treasury. This way the members will feel that the club or organization will benefit by their purchases as well as you, the entrpreneur. Be prepared with:

    a. A price list for each item.

    b. Have a theme, a reason, an occasion, etc.

    e. Offer the attendees something — a door prize, a discount, refreshments.

    f. A good idea would be to have a catalog listing each of the items with a price list and an order card attached.

    g. Get the names and addresses of every person attending, for your mailing list for FURTHER promotions and shows.

    h. Have an agenda. Keep control over the meeting or party. Direct the potential customer to what you want to sell.

    i. Don't let it drag on and on. Make it short, meaningful and informative. Then they will come again.

19. TRADESHOWS

NOTES

These are for the more experienced and successful entrepreneur. I receive many calls asking for advice. People have read my books or have attended my "How to Start a Home-made Business" seminars. Many of these callers want to know how productive it is to take their creations to a local or out-of-town trade show. Let's first define Trade Show. It could be a local home, craft, antique show, or whatever. The professionals call the displaying of like merchandise to interested buyers a Trade Show. Some may be just for wholesale selling, others may be oriented to the public. You have to make some decisions about this. There is a book that is published each year, listing just about every kind of show that is help in the U.S. It is called 19?? Exhibits Schedule, and is a directory of Trade and Industrial Shows. Write to Exhibits Schedule, 1518 Walnut St., Phila, PA 19102. In 1984 it was $85/year which included periodical supplements.

121

    1. Do you have enough products to sell at the show? Some attract tens of thousands of buyers.

    2. Can you generate enough profit to afford to attend the show? Some booths may rent for $400 and up.

    3. Can you afford the time away from business and family? Some go on for a week and more.

    4. Have you the stamina to "man" the booths? They may be open from 9 to 9 for 5 days . . . that's 12 hours per day. I spoke with a displayer of "Home-created butterfly/glass dome conversation piece," she stated that you don't eat or sleep normally and you have to be in good physical and mental condition. (Follow the basic rules listed under #1 "CRAFT SHOWS".)

20. SAMPLING

Many new and established products are promoted by sampling to certain areas of people. They then watch the product's acceptance by the orders the area retailers place. Sometimes they sell the product direct to the consumer. Some results are hard to judge. Ever see the sample packs of cigarettes given away on the street corner? They have a precluded outcome of this kind of sampling . . just how much good it will do for their brand of cigarettes. You cannot afford to give away many of your creations. I happened to be at a "Farmer's Market" yesterday. I passed a small donut-making stand. As I passed, someone handed me a small glazed donut. Of course I tasted it . . . I was hooked . . . I went back and bought a dozen, just because of that sample. I have seen this done with homemade candies, cheeses, etc. very effectively. Often your supermarket will have someone handing out fresh cooked "samples." Some liquor stores give taste samples of wine. Disney World's wine store has tasty samples to entice you to buy a large, high-profit bottle. What can **you** do?

a. Give samples to journalists who could write a good review about the product.

b. Give one to a prospective wholesaler buyer or distributor.

c. As a door prize to a craft show you are running.

d. To a disc jockey, celebrity who could "plug" your product.

e. To a receptionist at a show who could gently guide people to your booth.

f. As a bonus . . . buy one, get one free . . . buy two, get one free . . . buy one, get the second half price . . . etc.

g. As a raffle item to generate publicity for you or your product.

21. GOVERNMENT/INSTITUTIONS

Some people are making tons of money selling to governments and to institutions such as schools, hospitals, prisons and corporations. There is a book published called "SELLING TO THE U.S. GOVERNMENT." If you are serious about pursuing this kind of selling it would be a good idea to learn the "ropes" on how to sell to them. It is a different world, but can be very profitable. 'nuf said.

NOTES

122

22. TEACHING

This is a great way to spread your expertise and to build a reputation. I have been very successful using this method of merchandising. In fact, I think I taught first and became inspired from my students to under-take various business ventures. A good teacher, I always say, learns more than the students. Here are some ways to capitalize on your knowledge and skills:

1. Determine WHAT you are going to teach.

2. Make sure you know a lot more than you can teach.

3. Write down a plan for relating what you know to others — a "lesson plan" or a manual. (You can then sell the manual).

4. Make sure it is easy to follow and comprehensive.

5. Evaluate your skills at communicating. Can you influence others: Are your thoughts arranged in order? Can you hold the attention of an audience? Do you want to teach?

6. Determine how long it will take to "teach" the material you want to present. One, two, five or eight hours a week?

7. Investigate trying out at a community school adult education class. They are begging for classes that will attract the community. You might just have the one that will be well attended. Dale Carnegie started teaching at a local YMCA.

8. Find out if your local junior college, university, or trade school needs your class.

9. This is a good place to "test" different products and ideas.

10. This also is a good way to learn new methods and an excellent way to find out more about yourself.

11. It is another source of names and addresses.

12. You can give private lessons or consultations for a fee. I have found this to happen quite a few times.

13. This is a good way to find others with whom to "network."

14. It is a potential source for new friends.

You can teach by giving lessons, privately or at a craft store department store, etc. Many ceramic crafters combine their retail store sales with lessons. Communication is such a valuable tool. It can open many doors for you and your venture. If you are going to give lessons have a systemized procedure — i.e.:

1. Determine a price (by the hour, by the lesson etc.).

2. Set appointment times.

3. Determine if you are going to charge students if they miss a lesson. Many music teachers do charge if you miss.

4. Are you going to have a lesson manual?

NOTES

123

5. How many at a time — one, two 50, 100? When my wife Judy took "sketching" lessons relating to interior decorating, she took it with about ten others at the instructor's studio.

23. NEWSLETTER

Here's another good way to spread your name and information about your product. If you think you have enough to teach, communicate, review, research and relate to others, consider a newsletter. You should read a couple of books or newsletters on the subject of newsletters such as:

* Towers Newsletter . . . Jerry Buchanan, Box 2038, Vancouver, WA 98668,

* National Home Business Report . . . Barbara Brabec, Box, 2137, Naperville, IL 60566.

* Editing Your Newsletter . . . Mark Beach, Coast to Coast Books, 2934 NE 16th AVe., Portland, OR 97212.

You should have a source for names and addresses of people who would be interested in reading and subscribing to your publication.

NOTES

Try your first one. Have it typed up, Xeroxed at a Quick Printer and mail out 50-200. Enclose a subscription form and return envelope. If you get 2-5 subscriptions out of one hundred, you have a winner. There is a lot to the newsletter business, I would suggest doing some research and ivestigating before making a decision. Judy and I have had three newsletters, with only mild success. It takes a lot of promoting and up-front money to get enough subscribers to make it profitable.

For info on newsletters:
NEWSLETTER CLEARING HOUSE, 44 W-Markets, Box 311, Rhinebeck, NY 12571. Ask about Annual Directory of Newsletters.

124

24. SHOPPING GUIDES, PENNYSAVERS AND CLASSIFIED ADS

The reason why I include these sources of marketing is because they are relatively inexpensive. They reach a lot of potential buyers and are read thoroughly. This is in contrast to the placing of a "display" ad which costs a lot more and involves graphic, typesetting and layout costs. Display ads are placed wherever the paste-up person decides they will fit. They could be buried in a mass of other professional ads in the inside lower part of the page.

These low-cost advertising possibilities are good for "testing" the product, getting the feel of public acceptance with a little investment. You should:

1. Work and rework your ad until it looks excellent.

2. Remember that with these ads you get immediate response. The ad is usually placed within days rather than months when advertising in magazines and newsletters.

3. Every major buying decision anyone makes is first triggered by a strong emotional appeal such as:

   * SELF PRESERVATION
   * FAMILY
   * ROMANCE
   * MONEY
   * RECOGNITION

4. Aim at being specific about what you are offering in the least amount of words.

5. Avoid generalities. Don't say "How to buy 25 homemade crafts." Say "Hand crafted creations to make your home beautiful."

6. Reread your ad. Would you read it if it was among 100 similar ads?

7. Cut, cut and cut superfluous words.

8. Sell benefits to the reader. How can it help them be something, do something or look like something?

9. Many say that if you charge any more than $1 for an item in a classified ad you are wasting your money. There are exceptions but generally this media is used for testing or for gathering names and addresses to send a catalog or sales material later.

10. Offer an information package for $1. Barbara Brabec, author of Creative Cash, etc. tested a classified ad in FAMILY CIRCLE, I believe, and received thousands of replies. She then sent information about her newsletter and books.

11. If possible state that the dollar is refundable. This means they can deduct it from the first order. I usually send a "coupon" which states "this is worth $1 toward the purchase of any Success Publications items.

125

12. Try not to use a box number. People will respond to an address quicker.

13. Try to repeat the ad three times for best results.

14. Avoid listing a phone number. There are a lot of annoying people out there.

15. Try three different publications with three different ads and possibly three different prices.

16. Code your ads so you know where the responses are coming from.

17. Answer your responses immediately.

25. MANUFACTURER'S REP/SALESMAN

These are the people who could sell your goods to others. They in turn take part of the profit. They do a lot of business and move a lot of merchandise for some creators. They will insist on:

1. A price list for the consumer (to whom they are selling). If they are a successful sales house they may ask for more than you can afford to give.

3. You usually do the warehousing and shipping.

NOTES

4. Having promotional materials and samples to show customers.

5. Knowing your policies.

6. Inquiring if you give "datings."

7. A protected right to sell your product in a certain area. This means another "drummer" (salesperson) cannot sell it in the same area at the same time.

8. Knowing you pay the commission on receipt of the order or on the payment of invoice from the customer. (A good idea is to pay when you get paid. In that way any uncollected bills can be given to the salesperson to help collect.)

9. Follow up items that will sell as well as the first one. If you have a winner in the beginning, buyers are more apt to trust and buy from you again.

I had a book sales organization that caters to school libraries take my TEENAGE MONEYMAKING GUIDE. They did a fantastic job BUT took a large hunk of the profit. I talked to one small crafter who was waiting for a super large monthly magazine publisher to decide on her creation. It would be given away as a premium when ordering a subscription to the monthly. If chosen the order would be 150,000 units. Obviously she was quite concerned . . . it would change her whole operation from small to gigantic. Could she handle it? Could she produce it in enough time and with the same quality? (I cannot give details . . . it might effect the outcome.)

26. NETWORKING

This word is used a lot among craft, newsletter, and home-based business people. It means sharing your information, resources, etc. with another. It does not mean giving away all of your business secrets. "It does mean trying to help the other person." The golden rule. Every time I have given advice, addresses, resources, information to another compatriot, it has come back tenfold. There is a great "network" of enthusiastic enterprising people in our world. They emit a feeling of hope and excitement. Don't be afraid to give someone a compliment when you talk to them. Business can be a lonely job and "warm fuzzies" are few and far between.

Networking can save you hours of research. It can save you dollars in avoiding mistakes others have made. Share you knowledge with others. You will be surprised — someone may know something you don't. A newsletter is a form of "networking." The author/editor is sharing his knowledge and experience as well as others. A magazine is a commercial form of networking.

27. RADIO/T.V. ADVERTISING

These are terrific marketing tools, but I think that most of us should stay away. As you know it is very expensive and sometimes hard to measure the results. Unless you are asking for money to be sent, you will have a hard time measuring the ad's effect. This is done on the "blue ads" on late night TV. It is awfully hard to do on radio . . . very expensive. You may get some stations to announce your craft show if they have public announcements. The government states that they have to devote so many minutes or hours per week with these announcements, but they may air them at 3:00 a.m. These areas are for the pros.

NOTES

127

28. YELLOW PAGES

Most every city and town has some kind of telephone book advertising. I have seen towns with populations of under 1000 with ads in phone directories. If you are small and just starting out, phone book advertising should be in the future for you. When you become established and on the success road THEN you should list your company in the "yellow" pages. I would recommend just a listing at first, then advance to a larger ad. Unless you are doing hundreds of thousands a year, avoid the large display ads. Your authenticity will be strenghthened with just a listing. You must have a business phone in order to be listed. Ma Bell will not allow a residence phone to be listed under businesses. Yes, you're right, a business phone costs much more than your home phone.

29. TELE-MARKETING

This means selling or soliciting by phone. Here are some thoughts and information: (I like to number or letter my ideas. It seems to make things more organized easier to follow).

NOTES

a. You will have to write your "script" (it's much like writing an ad) of what you want to say.

b. Test your phone personality. Invest a few dollars in a device to attach to your phone. Plug this into a tape recorder and tape your phone conversation. As you play it back you will get a good feeling about your voice, "word whiskers," diction and clarity. Correct what you can improve on the others.

c. Determine how you will sell. Will it be C.O.D., personal delivery or Master/Visa?

d. Sell BENEFITS! BENEFITS! BENEFITS! Not that it is a well made, hand painted, beautiful ceramic statue of Ronald Reagan dancing with Queen Elizabeth, but a "sensuous" art to compliment your home.

e. Find a source of phone numbers. Many just go through the phone book one by one.

f. Be prepared to have many rejections. Some experts say 9 out of 10 will say no.

g. Always remain polite. You never know, their Uncle, boss or fellow groupie may buy from you.

h. Ask for referrals if they buy. "Is there someone else who would benefit from these eye-appealing statues for their front window?"

128

i. Ask for recommendations. It could be in letter form or verbal permission to use their name in future selling. Make sure you have a clear and positive statement AND inform them how you will use it.

j. If you find this to be successful, hire others to sell by phone. You can give them a percentage of what they sell. Newspapers rely on telemarketing to sell many subscriptions.

k. When you really get going, invest in a computer telemarketing device. The computer will dial the number, greet the responder, ask them questions, record the answers on a tape, disc or printout for you to review. It talks until it finishes a sentence then waits for an answer, when the responder's sentence is finished it turns back to the computer voice and asks another questions. It is voice activated. The answers can be recorded on a tape for you printed out on computer printer.

l. This is a tough job that requires persistence, follow through, patience and resistance to rejections.

NOTES

129

F. WHO CAN I SELL TO?

Listed here are over 100 places where you could possibly sell your products, patterns and ideas. I would suggest you make a form letter and send it to each of these companies. They may be interested in buying your creation(s). Many are buying patterns to re-sell to others.

1. Have a price list

2. Make sure your idea is protected with a copyright or patent. Most companies are honest, but we have to insure ourselves from those that are not.

3. Send a copy of one of your patterns with a cover letter.

4. Enclose a reply card and return envelope if possible.

Example: Good Morning:

Enclosed is one of my patterns/products. I would be interested in selling this to your company. Do you buy from independent artists? Please return the enclosed reply card. Thank you for your time and consideration.

NOTES

Judith Smith
8084 Nashua Dr.
Lake Park, FL 33410
(305) 626-4643

Reply card:

    I have received your letter and sample:

    _____ I am interested. Send price and details

    _____ Send more information

    _____ Call me at ( ) _____

    My name is _____

    _____ We are not interested, I am sending your sample back.

Name _____   Judith Smith
Company _____   8084 Nashua Dr.
Address _____ Phone ( ) Lake Park, FL 33410
State _____ Zip _____ (305) 626-4643

I have used this approach when soliciting reviews for my books. The reply card is almost always answered.

Have your material typed or photocopied in the most economical way.

A. NEEDLECRAFT AND FIBERARTS

American Crewel and Canvas Studio — P.O. Box 397, Nanuet, NY 10954. Threads, Fabrics, Supplies.

The American Needlewoman, Inc. — 3806 Alta Mesa Blvd., Century City 1 Shopping Center; Fort Worth, TX 76133. Kits: Latch hook, Needlepoint, Crewel and Embroidery.

Boye — A Newell Co., Freeport, IL 61032. Variety of Needlecraft items.

Columbia Minerva — Box 500, Robesonia, PA 19551. Needlepoint, Crewel and Cross-stitch kits.

The Craft Gallery, Ltd. — 100 Main St., Nyack, NY 10960. Fabrics, Hoops, Frames and Yarns.

Flying Fingers — P.O. Box 9197, Richmond Heights, MD 63117. Needlework kits.

The Heirloom Shop — 4300 N. State St., Jackson. MS 39206. Needlepoint ornament kits, Design books.

Herrschners Inc. — Hoover Rd., Stevens Pt., WI 54481. Needlepoint/Stitchery kits, Yarns, Frames and Fabrics.

Huning's Needlework — 201 N. Main St., St. Charles, MO 63301. Embroidery, Quilt and Fabrics.

The Knitting Etc., Corners — Box 494, Canfield, OH 44406. Needlepoint kits, Knitting kits, Sew/Quilt pillow kits.

Maryann's Creations — 10249 Glenoaks Blvd., Pacolma, CA 91331. Needlecraft kits.

Mary Maxim — 2001 Holland Ave., Port Huron, MI 48060. Knitting/Crochet sweaters kits, Holiday kits, Tools/Equipment.

The Needlecraft Shop — P.O. Box 2147, Canoga Park, CA 91306. Needlepoint canvas, Yarns, Tapestry Wools.

Straw Into Gold — 5533 College Ave., Oakland, CA 94618. Batik/Dyeing, Fabrics, Equipment, Dyes and Punch needle.

Suzicrafts — Box 706, Oak Park, IL 60303. Needlepunch sets, Yarn, Canvases, Fabrics.

Lee Wards — 1200 St. Charles Rd., Elgin, IL 60120. Kits, Yarns, Naturals, Ribbons, Miniatures.

Yarn N' Shuttle — 199 So. Highland at Poplar, Memphis, TN 38111. Macrame, Knitting/Crochet yarns.

DOLL AND TOY (SOFT)

All Dolled Up — P.O. Box 81, Kings Park, NY 11754. Doll dress pattern.

Audria's Crafts — 913 E. Seminary, Ft. Worth, TX 76115. Doll kit, Porcelain, Bisque "Crying Bi-Lo Baby."

Barbara's Patterns — 2309 Somerset, Castro Valley, CA 94546. Pattern 1800's doll w/ 9 outfits.

Bluegrass Babies — 596 Cherokee Rd., Raceland, KY 41169. Original patterns.

The Craft Tree — Hall Rd., Barrington, NH 03825. Doll parts, Doll kits, Animal eyes and Supplies.

El-Joy Cuddles — 668 East Ave., Lockport, NY 14094. Knitted toy patterns, Crochet toy patterns.

Kado Kits Inc. — P.O. Box 461, White Plains, NY 10602. Doll furniture kits.

Lady Bug — 4590 Via Vistosa, Santa Barbara, CA 93110. Doll clothes patterns.

NOTES

131

C. EMBROIDERY

C.M. Almy and Son, Inc. — 37 Purchase St., Rye, NY 10580. Yarns, Even weave cloth, Ecclesiastical supplies.

Art Etc. Studio — Rt. 1, Box 226 B, Wimberly, TX 78676. Cloth toddler doll patterns.

The Counting House — at the Hammock Shop, Box 155, Pawleys Island, SC 29585. Cross-Stitch kits.

Cross Stitch Corner — 2020 Central Ave., Augusta, GA 30904. Cross-stitch/Counted thread kits/Graphs.

Foxxie Stitchery — Box 224, Ridgewood, NJ 07451. Tools/ Equipment, Supplies, Fabrics.

Lurae's Creative Stitchery — P.O. Box 291, Bountiful, UT 84010. Pillow kits, Quilting kits, Patterns.

Renaissance Stitchery — P.O. Box 271, Port Alice, B.C., Von Zno, Canada. Renaissance Embroidery kits.

Jane Snead Samplers — Box 4909-B, Philadelphia, PA 19119. Sampler kits (embroidery)

Thumbelina Needlework Shop — 1685 Copenhagen Dr., P.O. Box 1065, Solvang, CA 93463. Embroidery fabrics.

KNITTING/CROCHET

Annie's Attic — Rt. 2, Box 212, Big Sandy, TX 75755. Designs/its, Crochet, Key chain doll patterns/Kits.

Annie's Knitting Patterns — Box 398, Chestertown, NY 12817. Knitting patterns book, Design graphs.

Golden Threads Knitting Studio — 1122 1960 — East, Suite D, Humble, TX 77338. Knitting patterns.

House of Chrisanca — P.O. Box 252, Corapolis, PA 15108. Quick crochet Christmas ornaments patterns.

Jan Knits — Box 315, Ingamar, MT 59039. Knitted sweater kits, Garmet kits.

Kits — Box 182, Madison Lake, MN 56063. Knitting kits.

NOTES

Knit-0-Graf Pattern Co. — 958 Redwood Dr., Apple Valley, MN 55124. Knitting patterns, "Magni Guide" magnifier wand.

Anne Lane Originals — Box 206, North Abington, MA 02351. Crochet patterns, Knitting directions.

M.D. & CO. — P.O. Box F., Youngstown, OH 44507. Crochet kits.

Margaret — 2934 N.E. 57th St., Portland, OR 97213. Crochet afghan patterns.

Mercury Enterprises — Box D-5, Fairhaven, MA 02719. Crochet patterns.

The Minaki Trading Co. — P.O. Box 63, Minaki, Ontario, POX 1JO, Canada. Quick Knit sweater patterns.

David Morgan — Box 70190, Seattle, WA 98107. Knitting Sweater Kits.

The Pattern People — Box 662, Northbrook, IL 60062. Knit/Crochet patterns.

Patternworks — Box 1690, Poughkeepsie, NY 12601. Knitting Sweater kits.

Schlund's — 3651 Pine Creek, Metamora, MI 48455. Crochet patterns.

Seabourne Publications — P.O. Box 15125, Winston-Salem, NC 27103. Crochet patterns for stuffed toys.

Sesler and Sons — P.O. Box 2054, Westminster, CA 92683. Crochet Flower kits.

Shelburne Spinners — North Ave. Extension, Burlington, VT. 05401. Knitting Kits, Hanspun yarns.

Sunwings, Inc. — 921 E. Port Susan Terrace Rd., Camano Island, WA 98292. Knit/Crochet kits.

MACRAME

Fiber Art — 10734 River Run Dr., Manassas, VA 22110. Macrame kits.

It' Knot Art — 106 Miry Brook Rd., Danbury, CT 06810. Macrame mirror/Wall hangings.

Knot Just Another Knotter — Dept. CS Box 613, Big Sandy, TX 75755. Macrame patterns/kits (exclusive).

Leisuretyme Crafts — P.O. Box 2225, 145 Sylvester Rd., So. San Francisco, CA 94080. Macrame kits.

NEEDLEPOINT

The Artifact — Box 57, Okahumpka, FL 32762. Needlepoint kits, Patterns.

Arts Array — P.O. Box 219, Calabasas, CA 91302. European Tapestry kits for petit point.

Eunice Beam — 5048 Northridge Place, Tucson, AZ 85718. Needlepoint kits.

Centerworked Needlepoint Specialties — 9945 Monroe, No. 207, Dallas, TX 75220. Centerworked needlepoint canvases.

Hand Dancers Needlepoint Design — Box 480, Northville, NY 12134. Needlepoint kits.

Handworks — P.O. Box 545, Smithtown, NY 11787. Needlepoint canvases/kits.

Hook and Needle — 31 Broadway, Rockport, MA 01966. Needlepoint kits.

The Idea Mill, Inc. — 40 Palisade Rd., Linden, N.J. 07036. Needlepoint kits.

Jan's Needleworks — Box 689, Old Bethpage, NY 11804. Needlepoint mug kits, Needlepoint footstool kit.

Magic Neelde Inc. — Mansard Square, 2200 Waukegan Rd., Glenview, IL 60025. Needlepoint kits/designs.

Mary McGregor — P.O. Box 154, Englewood, OH 45322. Needlepoint kits.

Needlecraft Creation by Joahne — P.O. Box 3132, Munster, IN 46321. Needlepoint kits.

Needlepoint Portraits — P.O. Box 9, Green Farms, CT 06436. Needlepoint Portrait kits. (from photograph).

Summerford Specialties — 925 So. Adams Ave., P.O. Box 61, Fullerton, CA 92632. Needlepoint purse kit.

Sunshine Designs — 4525 Sherman Oaks Ave., Sherman Oaks, CA 91403. Needlepoint kits.

Village Needlecraft — P.O. Box 2704, Chapel Hill, NC 27514. Needlepoint kits.

B.C. Wool Craft Ltd. — 512 West Hastings St., Van Couver, B.C., V6B 1L6, Canada. Needlepoint/Petit point kits.

G. QUILTING

Covered Bridge Fabricworks — Box 884, Flagstaff, AZ 86002. Good Feelings quilting kits.

Homecraft Services — 1441 Atlantic, Kansas City, MO 64116. Embroidered quilt designs.

Jensen's Custom Quilts — at the Treasure Chest, 41 N. 700 E. St. George, VT 84770. Quilt kits.

Kiddie Komfies — 15 SW 3rd. Ave., Ontario, OR 97914. Kiddie Komfies animal-shaped quilts patterns/kits.

Let's Quilt 'N Sew-On — Box 29526, San Antonio, TX 78229. Quilt patterns/kits.

Mary McGregor — P.O. Box 154, Englewood, OH 45322. Quilting graphs/kits with graphs.

Patch Arts — Box 765, Arapahoe No. 202, Boulder, CO 80302. Traditional quilt patterns.

Quilts and Other Comforts — Box 394, Wheatridge, CO 80033. Quilt kits, Pillow kits, Quilt patterns, Equip/Supplies.

NOTES

133

H. RUG MAKING

Lib Collaway Patterns —109 Shady Knoll Lane, New Canaan, CT 06840. Rug hooking designs.

The Crabtree Rug Studio — 121 Whipple Rd., Kittery, ME 03904. Rug hooking/braiding.

Craftsman Studio — North Street, Kennebunkport, ME 04046. Rug hooking equipment, Hooked rug designs.

Fallier Gallery — 10 Sawmill Dr., Westford, MA 01888. Rug hooking designs and supplies.

Heirloom Rugs — 28 Harlem St., Rumford, RI 02916. Hooked rug patterns.

Karlkraft Studio-Cheva — Severns Bridge Rd., South Merrimack, NH 030504. Rug hooking patterns.

Rittemere Crafts Studio, Ltd. — P.O. Box 240, Vineland, Ontario, LOR 2CO, Canada. Rug kit, Rug hooking designs.

Stitchin' Time — P.O. Box 18063—L, Rochester, NY 14618. Latch hook rug kits, Yarns accessories.

Wook Design, Inc. — 8916 York Rd., Charlotte, NC 28224. Latch hook rug kits.

Woolcraft, Inc. — North St., Medford, MA 02052. Latch hook rug kits, Needlepoint wools.

Yankee Peddler Hooked Rug Studio — 57 Saxonwood Rd., Fairfield, CT 06430. Rub hooking designs.

NOTES

I. SEWING

Judy Bean Crafts — P.O. Box 281, Kirbyville, TX 75956. Sewing kits/patterns.

Charing Cross Kits — Box 7992, Main St., Meredith, NH 03253. "Clothkit" sewing kits.

Country Mouse Patterns — P.O. Box 306, Mt. Freedom, NJ 07970. Sewing patterns, Holiday decorations.

Creative Makings by Martie — P.O. Box 4445, Glendale, CA 91202. Sewing patterns/accessories.

Frostline kits — Frostline Circle, Denver, CO 80241. 120 Sew-It-Yourself winter clothing project kits.

Jean Hardy Patterns — 2151 La Cuesta Dr., Santa Ana, CA 92705. Sewing patterns for clothing.

Kosmo Products — P.O. Box 501, Mt. Prospect, IL 60056. Sewing kits.

My Sister and I — P.O. Box 536, Montville, NJ 07045. Sewing Patterns for decorative items.

North Shore Farmhouse — Greenhurst NY 14742. Sewing kits, Potpouris, Calico fabrics.

Patchwork House — P.O. Box 891, Loveland, CO 80537. Tote bag patterns, Books.

The Pattern Patch — 12117 105th Ave., N.E., Kirkland, WA 98033. Sewing patterns, Fabric house plants, "Talking hand puppets."

Patterns — Box 11254, Honolulu, HI 96828. Hawaiian sewing patterns.

134

J. SPINNING/WEAVING

Dutch-Canadian Spinning Wheel Co., Ltd. — P.O. Box 70, Carleton Place, Ontario, KTC 3P3, Canada. "Louet" spinning wheel kits.

Ran Wools — 143 Smith St., Winnipeg, Manitoba, R3C 1J5, Canada. Weaving looms, Ram Spinner, Loom Project kits.

Rocky Road Crafts — Rt. 1, Rock Comfort, MO 64861. Loom making patterns.

Romni Wools and Fibers Limited — 3779 W. 10th Ave., Vancouver, B.C. V6R 265, Canada. Spinning wheels, Carding equipment, Weaving looms, Folkwear patterns.

Skil-Craft Corporation — P.O. Box 705, Racine, WI 53401. Loom weaving kit.

K. DOLL AND TOY (RIGID)

Build 'N Sew Patterns, Ltd. — Box 373, Lethbridge, Alberta, T1J 3Y7, Canada. Patterns for riding toys.

Creekside Creations — 3505 Bean Creek Rd., Scotts Valley, CA 95066. Marionette patterns/kits.

Mark Farmer Co., Inc. — 38 Washington Ave., Box 428, Point Richmond, CA 94807. Doll kits.

Larry Houston Studio — 2101 Estero Blvd., Ft. Meyers Bch., FL 33931. Old Fashioned Doll kits.

Sunshine Dolls — 2140 Sunnyside Pl., Sarasota, FL 33579. China doll kits.

The Sutler's Tent — Rt. 6, Box 270, Hartwood, VA 22471 Doll kits.

Connie Walton — 14171 Glitter St., Westminster, CA 92683. Doll kits, Porcelain parts, Human hair wigs.

Zielkraft — 112 N. Berteau, Bartlett, IL 60103. Doll kits, Service and Repairs by appointment.

Aprilz Apothecary, Inc. — box 111, Waterloo, NE 68069. Sachet kits.

Craft Creations — 4709 S.E. 86th Ave., Portland, OR 97226. Pods/cones/grasses - kits.

House of Hemp — 20250 Jeffers Dr., New Berlin, WI 53151. Sisal decorations kits.

NOTES

CHAPTER TEN

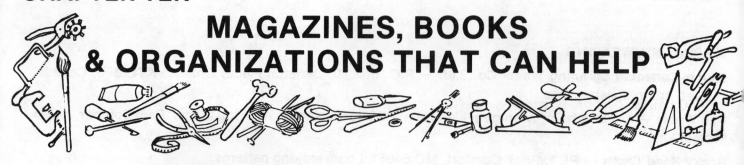

MAGAZINES, BOOKS & ORGANIZATIONS THAT CAN HELP

Listed are over 100 sources that you should consider. Write and ask for a review copy and their R&D information. They may be the media for you to advertise your product. They may give you invaluable ideas and short cuts. A subscription or purchase can save you lots of time and money. Most successful people do a lot of reading and research and have enormous libraries.

AMERICAN CRAFT - The American Craft Council, 22 W. 55th St., New York, NY 10019

ARTS AND ACTIVITIES — Publishers Development Corp., Suite 200, 591 Camino de la Reina, San Diego, CA 92108.

ARTS & CRAFTS NEWSLETTER — West Oak Hill Rd., Williston, VT 05495.

BEST IDEAS FOR CHRISTMAS — Woman's Day - $2.25, one a year, 200 N. 12th St., Newark NJ 07107.

BETTER HOMES & GARDENS NEEDLEWORK & CRAFT IDEAS — Published eleven times a year. Meredith Corp. 1716 Locust St., Des Moines, IA 50336.

BUTTERICK SEWING WORLD — Published four times a year, $6/year. Butterick 161 Avenue of the Americas, New York, NY 10013.

NOTES

BLACKSMITH GAZETTE — P.O. Box 1268, Mt. Vernon, WA 98273.

CANADA QUILTS — 360 Stewart Dr., Sudbury, Ontario P3E 2R8, Canada

CATALOG SOURCES FOR CREATIVE PEOPLE — 8084 Nashua Dr. Lake Park, FL 33410.

CEREMAIC WORLD — 429 Boren Ave., No., Seattle, WA 98109

CERAMICS MONTHLY — P.O. Box 12448, Columbus, OH 43212.

C.H.A.N. NEWSLETTER — Center for the History of American Needlework, Old Economy Village, 14th & Church Sts., Ambridge, PA 15003.

CHIP CHATS — National Woodcarvers Association, 7424 Miami Avd., Cincinnati, OH 45243

CHRISTMAS IDEAS — Better Homes and Gardens Creative Ideas, Published twelve times a year. Merideth Corp., 1716 Locus St., Des Moines, IA 50336.

COUNTED THREAD — 3305 So. Newport St., Denver, CO 80224.

CRAFT n' THINGS — Published six times a year, $7/year. Clapper Publishing, 14 Main St., Park Ridge, IL 60068.

CRAFT CONNECTIONS — Minneapolis Crafts Council, 528 Hennepin Ave., Minneapolis, MN 55403

CRAFT RANGE — Mountain-Plains Craft Journal, 6800 W. Oregon Dr., Denver, CO 80226

CRAFTS — News Plaza, P.O. Box 1790, Peoria, IL 61656

THE CRAFTS FAIR GUIDE — Box 262, Mill Valley, CA 94941

CRAFTS 'N THINGS — 14 Main St., Park Ridge, Il 60068.

THE CRAFTS REPORT — 700 Orange St., Wilmington, DE 19801.

CREATIVE CRAFTS — P.O. Box 700. Newton NJ 07860.

DECORATING & CRAFT IDEAS — P.O. Box C-30, Birmingham, AL 35283.

THE DECORATING PAINTER — P.O. Box 808, Newton, KS 67114.

DOLL CASTLE NEWS and THE DOLLMAKER — P.O. Box 247 — Washington, NJ 07882.

DOLL TIMES — P.O. Box 337, Oawego, IL 60543.

THE EGGER'S JOURNAL — 42 Colby Place, Philiplsburg, NJ 08865.

"ENJOY MACRAME" NEWSLETTER — 3817 No. Vermilion, Danville, IL 61832.

THE ENTERPRISING CRAFTSWOMAN and THE EXHIBITOR'S GUIDE TO CHICAGO AREA ART & CRAFT SHOWS — Daedalus Publications, Inc., 1153 Oxford Rd., Deerfield, IL 60015.

EXTRA INCOME — The home business magazine for women. Published bi-monthly (six times a year) $8.95. Box 2688, Boulder, CO 80322.

FAMILY CIRCLE — Published 17 times a year. 488 Madison Ave., New York, NY 10022.

FIBERARTS — 50 College St., Asheville, NC 28801.

FINE WOODWORKING — Box 355, 52 Church Hill Rd., Newtown, CT 06470.

FLYING MODELS — P.O. Box 700, Newton, NJ 07860.

GEMS AND MINERALS — Box 687, Mentone, CA 92359.

GLASS WORKSHOP — The Stained Glass Club, P.O. Box 244, Norwood, NJ 07648.

THE GOODFELLOW REVIEWS OF CRAFTS — P.O. Box 4520, Berkeley, CA 94704.

NOTES

GRANNY SQUARES & NEEDLEWORK — Published yearly by Women's Day, $2.25 CBS Publications, 1515 Broadway, N.Y., NY 10036.

THE HANDWORKER MAGAZINE — Rt. 1, Box 239, Wasaukee, WI 54177.

HANDWOVEN — From Interweave Press, 306 No. Washington, Loveland, CO 80537.

HOBBIES — THE MAGAZINE FOR COLLECTORS — 1006 So. Michigan Ave., Chicago, IL 60605.

INTERLOOP: THE KNITTERS AND CROCHETER'S ART — 1636 No. Twin Oaks Rd., San Marcos, CA 92069.

KNITTING MACHING NEWS & VIEWS — 315 Hamil Rd., Verona, PA 15147.

THE LOOMING ARTS — P.O. Box 233, Jordon Rd., Sedona, AZ 86336.

THE MALLET — National Carvers Museum, P.O. Box 389, Monument, CO 80132.

MAKE IT WITH LEATHER — P.O. Box 1386, Ft. Worth, TX 76101.

METALSMITH MAGAZINE P.O. Box 700, Newton, NJ 08760.

THE MINIATURE MAGAZINE — P.O. Box 700, Newton, NJ 08760.

MODEL RAILROADER — 1027 No. 7th St., Milwaukee, WI 53233.

MOTHER EARTH NEWS — 105 Stoney Mountain Rd., Hendersonville, NC 28739.

NATIONAL ART FAIR LIST — 300 So. 5th Ave., Minneapolis, MN 55415.

NATIONAL CARVERS REVIEW — Drawer 42693, Chicago, IL 60642.

NATIONAL HANDICRAFTER — Handicraft Press, Box 248, Grant Park, IL 60940.

NATIONAL HOME BUSINESS REPORT — Barbara Brabec, 8084 Nashua Dr., Lake Park, FL 33410.

NEEDLE ARTS — Embroiderer's Guild or America, 6 E. 45th St., Rm. 1301, New York, NY 10017.

NEEDLEWORK & CRAFTS — McCalls published six times a year, 825 7th Ave., N.Y., NY 10019.

NEEDLE & THREAD MAGAZINE — 4949 Byers, Ft. Worth, TX 76107.

THE NEEDLE PEOPLE NEWS — P.O. Box 115, Syosset, NY 11791.

NEEDLECRAFT FOR TODAY — 4949 Byers, Ft. Worth, TX 76107.

NEEDLEPOINT, INC. — P.O. Box 1585, Jupiter, FL 33458.

NEEDLEPOINT NEWS — Box 668, Evanston, IL 60204.

THE NEEDLEWORK TIMES — P.O. Box 87263, Chicago, IL 60680.

NUTSHELL NEWS — Clifton House, Clifton, VA 22024.

101 NEEDLEWORK & SWEATER IDEAS — Woman's Day, Published yearly. Woman's Day, 200 North St. Newark, NJ 07107.

ONTARIO CRAFT and CRAFT NEWS — Ontario Crafts Council, 346 Dundas St., W. Toronto, Ontario M5T 1G5, Canada.

ORNAMENT MAGAZINE — P.O. Box 35029, Los Angeles, CA 90035.

NOTES

PATCHWORK PATTER — National Quilting Association, P.O. Box 62, Greenbelt, MD 20770.

QUALITY CRAFTS MARKET — 521 Fifth Ave., Suite 1700, New York, NY 10017.

QUILT — Harris Publications, Inc., 79 Madiwon Ave., New York, NY 10016.

QUILTERS NEWSLETTER MAGAZINE — Box 394, Wheatridge, CO 80033.

RAILROAD MODEL CRAFTSMAN — P.O. Box 700, Newton, NJ 07860.

THE TUG HOOKER NEWS & VIEWS — Kennebunkport, ME 04046.

S. GAUGIAN — Model Railroad Magazine, 310 Lathrop Ave., River Forest, IL 60305.

SEW BUSINESS — Monthly publication, includes combination magazines with ART NEEDLEWORK and QUILT QUARTERLY, $15/year. 2100 N. Central Road, Box 1331, Ft. Lee, NJ 07024.

SEW NEWS — Box 10572, Des Moines, IA 50340, Monthly. $13.95/year.

SHUTTLE, SPINDLE & DYEPOT — Handweaver's Guild of America, Inc. 65 LaSalle Rd., P.O. Box 7-374, W. Hartford, CT 06107.

SPIN-OFF — 306 N. Washington, Loveland, CO 80537.

STITCH N' SEW — Published quarterly. $6 per year. House of White Birches, Box 337, Seabrook, NH 03874.

STUDIO POTTER — Box 172, Warner, NH 03278.

TOLE WORLD — 429 Boren Ave., No., Seattle, WA 98109.

TOLEFINDER — 2710 Moonriver, Dallas, TX 75234.

TREADLEART — 2458 W. Lomita Blvd., Suite 223, Lomita, CA 90717.

VOGUE PATTENS — Published six times a year. $10.95/year. 161 Avenue of the Americas, N.Y., NY 10013.

THE WEAVER JOURNAL — Colorado Fiber Center, Inc. P.O. Box 2049., Boulder, CO 80306.

WOMEN'S CIRCLE — The Nationwide Friendly Homemakers Club. Published bimonthly, $6/year. House of White Birches, Box 335, Seabrook, NH 03874.

THE WORKBASKET — 4251 Pennsylvania Ave., Kansas City, MO 64111.

WORKBENCH — 4251 Pennsylvania Ave., Kansas City, MO 64111.

AMERICAN CRAFT — American Craft Council, 22 W. 5th St., N.Y., NY 10019.

AYER DIRECTORY OF PUBLICATIONS — 210 W. Washington, Sq., Phil., PA 19106.

DIRECTORY OF PUBLISHING, BRADFORD MT. BOOK ENT., — 125 East 23rd St., N.Y., NY 10010 — cover's the U.K and Common Wealth.

FINANCIAL CONTROL FOR THE SMALL BUSINESS, COLTMAN, TAB BOOKS — Summitt, PA 17214.

HANDCRAFTS THE HANDICAPPED ELDERLY CAN MAKE AND SELL — Russell, C.C., Thomas, 2600 So. First St. Springfield, IL 626717.

HOMEMADE MONEY — "BRABEC" — Success Publications, 8084 Nashua Dr., Lake Park, FL 33410.

HOW TO START & OPERATE A MAIL ORDER BUSINESS — $24.95 in book stores and libraries, by Julian Simon.

LITERARY MARKETPLACE, THE DIRECTORY OF AMERICAN BOOK PUBLISHING, — R.R. Bowker, 205 E. 42nd St., N.Y., NY 10017.

MAIL ORDER MOONLIGHTING — Cecil Hope, $7.95, A classic in its field, Book stores and libraries.

NATIONAL CALANDER OF THE INDOOR/OUTDOOR ART FAIRS — 5423 New Haven Ave., Ft. Wayne, IN 46803.

198? EXHIBITS SCHEDULE ANNUAL DIRECTORY OF TRADE AND INDUSTRIAL SHOWS — 1518 Walnut St., Phil., PA 19102.

SEWING FOR PROFIT — $10.00, Success Publications, 8084 Nashua Dr., Lake Park, FL 33410.

SATANDARD RATE & DATA — Consumer Magazine and Agrimedia.

TEENAGE MONEYMAKING GUIDE — 101 ways teens can earn their own money. $10.00 — Success Publications, 8084 Nashua Dr., Lake Park, FL 33410.

THE INTERNATIONAL DIRECTORY OF LITTLE MAGAZINES, AND SMALL PRESSES — Dust Books, Box 100, Paradise, CA 95969.

THE SEW AND SAVE SOURCE BOOK — Success Publications, 8084 Nashua Dr., Lake Park, FL 33410.

NOTES

NOTES

CHAPTER ELEVEN
MEASURING RESULTS OF MY EFFORTS

ANYTIME you produce a product, place an ad, run a promotion, have a sale, exchange money, materials and goods you should have a system to record the transactions. We suggest that you have a plan and a budget. This is one way to measure results. If you do or don't achieve your goal or if you spend more or less money than you have, then you have the results. What other ways can we measure to make our business more professional and successful?

NOTES

1. A PLAN, a set of goals, a direction. Airplane pilots must file a flight plan with the authorities. This tells where they are going, by what route, estimated time of departure and estimated time of destination arrival. You must also file a flight plan — a set of tasks that must be done before you reach your destination or goal(s).

2. A BUDGET. How much do I have, how will it be spent and for what? This measures the money flow.

3. PERSONAL GOALS. What do YOU want to achieve with this undertaking? This measures where you are going in relationship to the business.

4. A BUSINESS LEDGER. A book containing expenses, accounts receivable, accounts payable, cash transactions, etc. This measures WHAT the business is doing.

5. A REVIEWS TRACKING CHART. (See example.) This will measure responses from reviewers. If they have answered, when to follow through etc. This measures what other think of your product.

6. ADVERTISING TRACKING CHART. (See example B) This will measure the responses to "coded" mailings or advertisements.

7. PRODUCT SCHEDULE. I have a 1 x 4 gummed label on the top of my typewriter. I record the date and how many papers of the current book I am writing. It gives me a sense of satisfactioin if I am writing the 6 pages a day I must produce. It also shames me when I fall behind.

8. A LIST OF CUSTOMERS AND INQUIRERS. Many times I have suggested you should save all names and addresses that you can for future promotions and mailings. This measures your potential market and existing customers.

NOTES

9. A DAILY TO-DO LIST. Every day you should make list of what you want to accomplish for that day. It measures how effective you can be . . . it gives you a kick in the butt when you get lazy (it does me). I reward myself with a treat if I get the list done. If I don't, I add the undone to tomorrow's list. (I also save mine. Handy if you have forgotten to save a name, address or phone number).

10. AN APPOINTMENT BOOK. Obviously this means how you can spend your time.

11. A BANK BOOK. This means what you got and what you ain't got.

12. A MAIL-OUT LIST. I jot down who I am mailing something to each day, (not by bulk mailings). This measures your areas of accomplishments, by mail.

14. Some have a PHONE LOG. Like a mailing log, this records and measures with whom and when you communicated via the phone. Some offices insist on this to regulate personal and long distance calls.

15. A BOOK LIST. A slip of paper where you record the books you have read. This measures that thirst for knowledge. I set a goal of so many books per year. I have kept a record for the last twenty years. Takes about 10 minutes/year.

16. A FILING SYSTEM. This will measure the information and sources you want to save for future use. It should be systematic and filed alphabetically.

17. A TICKLE FILE. Record what you have to do in the near future, correspondence waiting for an answer, bills that you want paid, projects you want to start. I look at mine once a month, it gives a great measure of "did I do it, or did they do it?"

18. AN INDEX OF BOOKS and a brief explanation. A measure of what books you have in your library.

Some of these may seem inappropriate to your way of doing things. You may have other ways of measuring like a weight chart, exercise chart, calorie counter etc. It is important to be organized. It is another door opening to success.

19. AN INVENTORY. Count and price all of your materials and finished products. A measure of what your Business/Inventory is worth.

NOTES

NOTES

CHAPTER TWELVE

NOW WHERE?

I have reviewed the essential tools needed to market and sell your creation. If you have done most of these and have achieved a measure of success . . . what now? We humans are much like the green plants in our yards. They are either growing or dying. A business is much like this. You cannot stand still and do the same amount of business you did last year. With inflation, the increased costs of materials and labor you'd be falling behind.

A. SELLING YOUR CREATION OR BUSINESS

You may have reasons to divest yourself of the business or sell the rights, patent, copyright or your creation. Many times you can earn healthy profit from your hard work. How do you go about it?

NOTES

1. Set a price on the business or product. There are as many formulas as there are accountants. Figure how much inventory you have at cost (including equipment). You may want to take three years profits added on to the inventory to come up with a ball-park figure to charge!

2. Decide if you want to carry money or a mortgage. You will find many buyers out there with very little cash to put down but full of promises. In my many years of buying and selling business, take this advice. GET AS MUCH DOWN AS YOU CAN. If you have to carry a balance then secure it with some kind of collateral that you can "grab" if they fail or renege. Many, many, many times a person will fail at the business and end up owing the originator A LOT OF MONEY.

3. The New Owner may want you to stay on as an advisor. If they do, charge a fee, or make it part of the selling price.

4. Be prepared to sign a NON COMPETE clause. This would state that you could not make, sell, represent, etc. the business or a similar business or product withing a certain area (a city, county) for so many years. In other words, you could not open across the street and be in competition.

5. Make sure the buyer knows what she/he is doing. Do they know anything about your products or do they just see the dollar bill signs? Be very cautious, investigate; don't let all that work go down the drain.

6. Make double sure you want to sell and get out. You may want to take and investor (inject capital — or a partner, you may want to sell shares of stock.

B. EXPANDING

1. To expand you should be successful with what you are selling now.

2. Examine products that are similar, can enhance or be a companion to yours.

3. Most successful businesses have MULTIPLES to sell. As soon as you feel that your first line of products is selling well, be ready with additional items.

4. Be sure you need that extra person. It means additional record keeping, payroll records, taxes, etc. You might be considering paying them "under the counter" or not taking out taxes. Here are some of the disadvantages of paying without deducting taxes.

   a. They can become injured on the job and sue you for medical expenses.

   b. If they become angry or mad at you, they can go to the labor board and "turn you in." This means you could be liable for ALL back taxes AND penalties and interest charges.

NOTES

   c. You will not be able to use this payroll expense as a deduction on your income tax report.

   d. The person has no proof that they ever worked.

   e. If enough people find out, others may "blow the whistle on you."

5. You may employ two or less people and not have to take out workman's compensation.

6. When you put that extra person(s) to work, DON'T give away your business secrets. I have seen many "copy cats," those who STEAL ideas from others while they are working. One of our friends, Jerry Buchanan of the Towers Club Newsletter, advises that as soon as we publish a book we should promote it like mad. He states that here are many who will steal or copy a successful book.

7. When I was in the pharmacy business I learned from an old wise druggist something that has lasted in my mind for years, "NEVER LET THEM KNOW BUSINESS IS GOOD. SOMEONE WILL OPEN ACROSS THE STREET FROM YOU. TELL THEM IT COULD BE BETTER." It's hard not to brag or tell the world of your successes, BUT it pays to keep it to yourself or to your trusted loved one.

8. You don't need partners, you need helpers!

9. Test any added ideas BEFORE investing a lot of time and money.

10. Construct a procedure plan, a budget and a projected sales estimate.

11. Do you have enough capital, expertise, equipment, finances and time to do a good job?

12. Do your homework and prepare well.

146

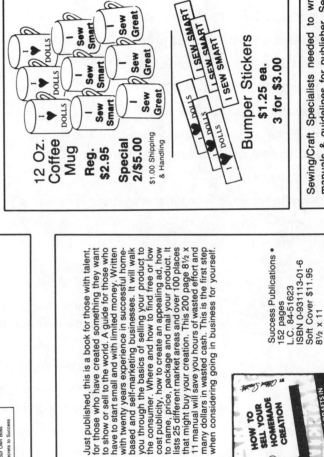